S0-AKG-388

Tragedy of Riches

Tragedy of Riches

Stephen Barber

University of Buckingham Press

First published in Great Britain in 2011 by

The University of Buckingham Press
Yeomanry House
Hunter Street
Buckingham MK18 1EG

© Stephen Barber

The moral right of the author has been asserted.

All rights reserved. No part of this publication may be
reproduced, stored or introduced into a retrieval system or
transmitted in any form or by any means without the prior
permission of the publisher nor may be circulated in any form of
binding or cover other than the one in which it is published and
without a similar condition including this condition being
imposed on the subsequent purchaser.

A CIP catalogue record for this book is available at the British
Library

ISBN 9780956395238

For Maria

Stephen Barber is Senior Lecturer at London South Bank University where he teaches on its leading MPA programme. He is a fellow of the Royal Historical Society and Senior Fellow at the Global Policy Institute. A regular commentator in print, on radio and television, he has published four previous books.

Contents

Foreword i

Introduction 1

1) The Second Decaders 7

2) The Origins of Our Riches 25

3) The Mixed Economic Settlement 49

4) Decades of Acceptance 81

5) The Death of Domestic Policy 105

6) The Unsustainable Cheat.............................. 137

7) Our Age of Anxiety...................................... 181

8) Hardship and Rejuvenation 209

Conclusion: A Challenge to Politics.................. 235

Afterword 237

References 241

Index..261

Riches do not consist in the possession of treasures but in the use made of them.

Napoleon Bonaparte

The greatest good you can do for another is not just to share your riches but to reveal to him his own.

Benjamin Disraeli

Foreword

As this book was in its final stages, violent riots broke out in numerous London boroughs and subsequently in other English cities. Shops were looted, cars and property vandalised and arson raised buildings to the ground. Half of those arrested were under eighteen and many remained unrepentant, even proud of their actions. The lawlessness was greeted with shock and eventually political determination. But amid the coverage, debate and discussion which reverberated around the world, there was bewilderment as to why this had happened in a wealthy and stable democracy such as Britain. These pages will not address the reasons behind the riots but the intellectual fallout of events feeds directly into many of the themes of this book. These include excess, selfishness, entitlement, political malaise and undefined visions. It also contextualises the more uncertain world in which we find ourselves this side of the great recession.

Europe and the United States breathed a sigh of relief as the world economy recovered post credit crunch and it seemed that our great riches, greedily accumulated over six decades, would be protected. But this only served to underline our misplaced faith in a system which is now ill-equipped to deal with our real needs in the second decade of the twenty first century.

Offering a critical analysis of our political system, this book argues that politicians over the past twenty years have squeezed our economic destiny and that the corresponding demise of ideology means that we have reached the limits of what can now be achieved without fundamental political change. The book introduces the concept of the 'mixed economic settlement'; the argument that the policy mix in which Europe and the United States operates is forged in three contrasting forms of liberalism to have emerged in the post-war West: economic, welfare and social liberalism. The purpose of this settlement is disintegrating and the book makes a passionate case that instead of the complacency of the last two decades we now need a new, political, settlement prepared to tackle the great issues of our age and once again broaden our economic destiny, before it is too late.

The book describes how our single minded pursuit of prosperity has constrained politics from being a force for good. It demonstrates just how rich we are but asks why the capitalist visions of the 1950's and 1960's did not turn into a Utopia in the second decade of the twenty-first century. Instead we are faced with social dysfunction and widespread dissatisfaction ; a political system often incapable of reconciling competing demands.

The book argues that our present policy prescriptions are unsustainable and, if we are to tackle the big and difficult issues of the new decade, politics and communities alike need to face up to this truth.

This is meant to be a provocative book which follows the baby boomers as they take full advantage of the golden age of capitalism and assume the political reigns. It follows the development of the mixed economic settlement, arguing that it was cemented by those baby boomers as they formed the most pragmatic of governments at the end of the cold war and shows that the new post baby boom generation of politicians are even more alike, more global in their outlook and even less ideologically driven. Their approach is flawed.

The credit crunch has so far represented a missed opportunity to rejuvenate policy. But it is clear that a new post-majoritarian politics, where sustainable partnerships are formed across the political spectrum and driven up from communities, is essential. The book now lays down a challenge to the current generation of politicians and communities to boldly complete the mixed economic settlement project with a fundamental change to the way we do politics.

Stephen Barber, 2011

Introduction

You are rich but you could have so much more. And chances are you wish you had.

In the last two decades politicians of all parties and across the democratic world have colluded with voters to limit our economic destiny. Not in terms of the amount we have, which is unlimited, but rather what we do with it. It is unsustainable and if we are to tackle the big and difficult issues of the new decade, politics and communities alike need to face up to this truth.

We live in a bubble of economic prosperity that separates us from the poverty of the recent past and the poorest parts of the world today. We have rarely been richer or more deeply immersed in consumerism and consumption. And as the response to the global financial crisis demonstrates, with its banking bail out and massive fiscal stimulus, the economic power of the Western world is profound. Why is it then, in the rich second decade of the twenty-first century, that we do not live in some sort of advanced paradise? Why is it that our societies are dysfunctional and its people so dissatisfied? The tragedy of our riches is that the great wealth we have created since the Second World War has not created greater happiness or wellbeing; it has not supported political participation or reconciled conflicting political demands; it has not defended policymaking against the ravages of globalisation. Indeed, the tragedy is that our riches are a cause of our greatest problems.

This is not an anti capitalist book. It does not sit comfortably in the tradition of numerous publications to emerge over the past decade or so from the likes of Naomi Klein, Michael Hardt, Slavoj Zizek, George Monbiot, Mark Fisher and even the more mainstream Soros and Stiglitz – although it might share a readership. While this book describes the often dysfunctional nature of our modern economies, political systems and contemporary societies, it neither advocates some sort of neo-Marxist response nor does it gaze back fondly to a golden age that never was. This book starts with the propositions that we are all capitalists now (and probably always were), and financially at least, have done rather well over the past six or so decades from a pretty effectively operating capitalist system. But it also laments the tragedies of the single minded pursuit of riches which has characterised policy making since the last decade of the twentieth century and argues that capitalism can deliver far more in terms of successful politics, civil society and wellbeing if only there were the will of both politics and society. In this respect too, it differs from the usual panacea of more state intervention, regulation and control. The case is made that initiatives, if they are to be successful, need to be forged in sustainable and broad partnerships across party politics and driven up from communities.

This is a book about public policy and it is a book about our political economy. But it is not a book set in abstract. It is concerned with the way we live our lives today, how we enjoy the riches we have accumulated and the tragedy of the sort of societies they have created. And it is about how politics is coordinated and policy made. In terms of how we respond, it is more inclined towards political resolutions and regenerated visions than dusty economics.

Part political theory, part history, part economy, this book follows the baby boomers as they enjoy the fruits of the golden age of capitalism and eventually assume political office. And by introducing the concept of the 'mixed economic settlement'

- the argument that the policy mix in which Europe and the United States operates is forged in three contrasting forms of liberalism to have emerged in the post-war West: economic, welfare and social liberalism - it argues that this settlement was cemented as the baby boomers formed governments at the end of the cold war but it also blames this generation for limiting the ambitions of what we do with our riches and for failing to develop a political strand to the project. And it shows now that the post baby boom generation of politicians that follow are far more alike, more global in their outlook and even less ideologically driven.

Acknowledging the power of globalisation and markets, it nonetheless demonstrates that the great demographic and technological changes mean that conflicting political demands need to be reconciled. The book argues that in the last decade of the twentieth century and the first decade of the twenty first, the mixed economic settlement became broadly cemented into public policy. But these two post ideological decades were also responsible for the tragedy of our riches as seen in political failure and dysfunctional societies. The book offers a critical analysis of our political discourse and argues that the settlement is an incomplete project which has allowed for our malaise and now represents a challenge to the politics which has sustained it. It is a story of what has gone right, what has gone wrong and what now needs to be done.

Along the way, readers will find short pen portraits of key political and social figures, national and provincial, each of which has helped shape the world in which we live today, giving flavour and texture to a story which involves us all. Alongside political leaders such as Margaret Thatcher, Ronald Reagan, Tony Blair, Bill Clinton and George W. Bush, stand Huey Long, Joseph Stiglitz, Eleanor Roosevelt and John Maynard Keynes.

The book acknowledges the emerging belief that public policy directed primarily towards economic growth has not improved society or wellbeing in our advanced world but questions the ideas of entitlements and happiness economics where unproductive, hedonistic outcomes might be no better. In contextualising the debate in the global economic crisis, the book argues that the credit crunch represented a missed opportunity to rejuvenate policy, adding a strand to the mixed economic settlement. But that the overt prescriptions of the industrialised world, single-mindedly focussing on growth, means that amid the hardship of recovery, many will question whether broader aims, including developing greater societal sense of common purpose, might not be weaved into policy.

With a British author, this book quite naturally is grounded in Britain and more broadly the European experience. But it is outward looking to America and other rich societies of today which have grown in the European tradition across the world. The story this book tells is one which is familiar to Western and Western style democratic economies. The book, however, concentrates on the complementary experiences, policy, politics and outcomes of the United States of America on one side of the Atlantic and Britain and Western Europe on the other. For it is the people of these two continents, to varying degrees, who embody the tragedy of our riches.

This is a book which attempts to understand just where we are in the second decade of the twenty-first century and where we might be headed. It does this by drawing together numerous political, economic and policy debates in eight chapters and numerous sub-chapters. Each of these chapters could be topics for books themselves as could several of the sub chapters which could have been expanded greatly. In being disciplined about the depth this book is able to engage in such debates, it has inevitably left much unexplored. But in bringing them together, it is hoped that a coherent narrative has been formed upon which discussion and debate can be built.

It is hoped too that this book offers not only insights into the world that we have created from political, economic and historical perspectives but that it is also able to point the way for the priorities of policy makers as they form strategies for the coming years and decades. In this sense it is optimistic. We have created powerful open economies capable of ingenuity and wealth creation. Re-deployment of this power need only be a matter emphasis. But it requires broader visions of what a rich society can achieve for its own peoples and the world. And it needs us all to be more honest about the conflicting choices before us.

Chapter One

The Second Decaders

Both Producers Research and High-Grade Living Declare
He was fully sensible to the advantages of the Instalment Plan
And had everything necessary to the Modern Man,
A phonograph, a radio, a car and a Frigidaire.
Our researchers into Public Opinion are contest
That he held the proper opinion for the time of year;
When there was peace he was for peace when there was war he went.
He was married and added five children to the population,
Which our Eugenist says was the right number for a parent of his
generation.
Was he free? Was he Happy? The question is absurd:
Had anything been wrong, we should certainly have heard.[1]

W.H. Auden had an idea of how the ideal citizen should behave. His satire, published in 1939, eulogises the memory of one of us whose conduct was impeccable in the eyes of the state. A standardised, modern and average life measured by official statistics; an anonymous number amid a collective, his individualism buried. Written so long ago, these lines remain spookily poignant. They reflect the pressures and expectations of life in the second decade of the twenty-first century perhaps even more so than they did on the eve of the Second World

War: pressures to own and to consume; pressures of policy to please opinion; demographic and technological pressures; the careless assumption that our world makes us happy; and the tension between the state and its people.

But in the second decade of the twenty-first century, we seem to have very little to complain about in the industrialised world, dominated by the economic blocs of the United States on the one side of the Atlantic and Europe on the other. Despite the global economic crisis being a raw memory, we have very few wants and have amassed great riches by any fair comparison. Unhappily, the wealth we have generated over the decades since Auden wrote the poem have not given us the sort of world which many predicted a generation or so ago.

Britain and the United States, it was once said by George Bernard Shaw, were 'two countries separated by a common language' and there is some truth in this as is the tangible tensions between modern European world views and those of America. But these differences, so stark when viewed from home, all but disappear when observed from those parts of the world with very different experiences of life. Europe and the United States not only share a history but also share a philosophical approach to politics, policy and society. In the twenty-first century, European and American divisions might seem sharper but it is only the absence of an identifiable common threat or enemy which serves to overstress our disparity. After all, when they emerge, whether in the guise of ideological terrorism or banking meltdown, there is palpable solidarity and a commonality of response. This chapter considers life, politics and society for Europeans and Americans in this young decade. It explores attitudes and lifestyles which have been afforded by consistent, yet narrow, capitalist policy making and the creation and maintenance of riches rarely seen before in expansive society. But at its heart this chapter observes the capitalist vision from the past, which looked to a brighter future, and wonders if we have not limited the destiny which is now our present.

Why Economics is Key

Industrialised trade, capital and markets matured in Europe and the United States of America. And since the Second World War, it is the peoples of these two giants who have enjoyed the fruits of its success, immersed in a fortunate prosperity and freedom like few other people on earth. Economic growth has been steady and consistent. Real GDP per person grew at 4.06% per year between 1950-1973 in (the 16 countries of) Western Europe and 2.45% in the USA. And from 1973-2005 figures came in at 1.86% and 1.91% respectively. Europe in particular, grew historically rapidly during the years after 1945, in part representing recovery from the destruction of war and in part recovery from the depression of the 1930s which affected the States so terribly too. Taking a much longer view, GDP per person in 2005 Europe was 'about ten times the ten level in 1870.'[2] But the prosperity of Europe and the United States have been interlinked, with the latter providing technology and trade liberalisation within and between these blocs adding significantly to our riches.[3] Furthermore, the prosperity created has been more than chance. As the economists Nicolas Crafts and Gianni Toniolo demonstrate in their analysis of Western European growth, 'microeconomic foundations matter for growth so institutions and policy make a real difference.'[4] Policy making has not only been successful, but the prosperity of Europe and the United States has also been interdependent.

The strength, or indeed necessity, of the transatlantic economic relationship was obscured for most of the post war period during which the fear of nuclear destruction, a common enemy and security interests coordinated by NATO characterised diplomacy.[5] Indeed even the more recent so-called war on terror proved more enticing for global leaders. But as Henning Meyer has argued, 'the transatlantic marketplace is by far the most important one in the world today. And the EU and the US rarely miss an opportunity to stress their joined cultural heritage and shared commitment to economic and political values. Additionally, economic interests seem to be converging in view of rising competition from emerging economies'[6]. That is, transatlantic economics is central to the relationship between Europe and the States in the second decade of the twenty first century and central to the ongoing prosperity of its peoples. And in trade discussions, the subtle differences between these two blocs' approach to economic and social management are apparent in a way in which diplomatic differences were vague during cold war.

Europhiles and proponents of America alike will cheer their own side's interpretation of capitalism. For Europeans, it is a 'social market' which distinguishes its creed, a central feature of EU economies typified by Germany, France and Scandinavia (some of which sits outside the Union). It embodies greater welfarism and recognition of worker rights. In the USA, the freedom of capital is more intense, hiring and firing easier but charity and giving far greater. At ground level then, there is 'a social and economic order for Europeans that breaks with the American *idée fixe* about the free market… it believes that Europeans, whilst not abandoning the profit motive or private ownership, can provide for much more equality and social civility than does the US model.'[7] There are greater social protections and state provision of services evident in Europe; perhaps greater opportunities to innovate and create jobs in the USA. The result is that America tends toward the individual while Europe leans in the direction of the collective. This means that in healthcare, say, Europe might offer more consistent levels of provision for all its people but the best and most cutting edge medicine will be found in the States. There are differences and similarities and we can learn from each other. But this is a view perhaps only seen from the ground. From the air, we are not so different.

The Social Democratic Contradiction

The differences between the United States and Europe are not inconsiderable. But they have been exaggerated. Both are capitalist economies forged in industrial production and global expansion. As John Kay put it 'France and the United States are rich countries. The United States grew more rapidly than France in the 1990s after four decades in which the opposite was true. GDP per head in the USA is about 20 per cent higher than in France, but French working hours are about 20 per cent shorter than in the USA, so that hourly output is much the same in the two countries. From a statistical perspective, the difference between the two countries is that the French take lunch and five weeks' holiday.[8] These are convinced capitalist economies whose public policy differs somewhat. But for different reasons, Europe and America sought refuge in political language reflective of their experiences. That word, 'capitalism' has come to be (and has long been) used as a derogatory term. For some, to be a capitalist is to be immoral, to be selfish, to be greedy.[9] And yet which mainstream politician is not a capitalist?

11

We live in openly capitalist societies: capital is on the whole privately owned and controlled. Fortunes can be made and lost; there are property rights and open markets. While taming the wilder excesses of capitalism has been a task which has long bedevilled governments of all creeds, supporting capitalism is at the heart of most governments' programmes across the world today. Just look at the global response to the 2008 economic downturn. Amid the criticism of the system and the vilified actors, the solid consensus was to 'save capitalism'. But that does not stop some at the very centre of our politics from wincing at the very term. And even those hailing from political traditions drawn from the capitalist classes prefer a more sedate language. Indeed the stampede to rediscover Keynesianism in the wake of the credit crunch, as if this were some leftist creed, is perplexing given that the great economist was the most pragmatic of capitalists who was 'quite happy to promote luxury and waste as ways of sustaining economic growth. He believed that thrift was dysfunctional, but greed was good if it boosted demand and prevented recession.'[10] It did not strengthen any anti-capitalist values in mainstream politics, and only served to fortify the idea of the centralised, interventionalist state.

For the great economist J.K. Galbraith, there are historical reasons for this reaction. Organised capitalism emerged in the late nineteenth century and became associated in Europe with the power imbalance between the dominant owners of the means of production and the sometimes oppressed workers. In the United States it became associated with another form of exploitation as the great monopolists of Rockefeller, Carnegie and Duke to name but three exerted their powers over prices. Capitalism was implicated as an origin of war in 1914 and by the time of the great depression in the 1930s, it had truly besmirched its reputation. And so, in the post 1945 war world, the hunt was on, not for a better system, but for a better form of words. Galbraith:

In Europe there was 'Social Democracy' – capitalism and socialism in a compassionate mix. In the United States, however, socialism was (and it remains) unacceptable… So in reasonably learned expression there came 'the market system.' There was no adverse history here, in fact no history at all. It would have been hard, indeed to find a more meaningless designation – this a reason for the choice.[11]

The widespread antipathy directed towards the concept of capitalism masks the reality that most of us are capitalists. And yet as an ideology, capitalism is not one to which many would actively subscribe or to enthusiastically man the barricades of its dogma. It perhaps explains another positive word plucked from our language. 'Freedom' was a favourite word of President George W. Bush, and to a lesser extent Tony Blair, to justify the wayward foreign policy adventure which began after 9/11. Freedom, not capitalism, is the near unobjectionable term employed to imply the promotion of democracy. We might not think ourselves to be capitalists but surely we believe in freedom. Policy with freedom at its core is bound to elicit popular support and indeed, notwithstanding the Iraq war, over decades it has. But it is difficult to argue that US foreign policy has been directed towards the altruistic support of democracy. Rather, it has been 'to make the world safe for capitalism' (or as Henry Kissinger once remarked, 'America has no permanent friends only interests'). And most of us in the West benefit from a world which is safe for capitalism even where we despair of its excesses.

Nevertheless, as Guy Sorman put it in his infamous article, the 'free market still has enemies and critics, ranging from those who dream of a world more just, more spiritual, or transformed in some other utopian way to those who simply seek to defend their own narrow material interests. And we must not overlook ignorance: economic principles aren't widely understood among the public or even among lawmakers.'[12] It is also why the soft left choose to imbue the term 'neo-liberal' to distinguish their brand of capitalism from the 'real capitalists'. Anti-capitalists today are left in a similar quandary. John Kay observes the mood when he points out the success of anti-globalisation books written by the likes of Monbiot, Klein and Hutton. He also notes the 2001 May Day protestors in London, one 'carried a placard 'Capitalism should be replaced by something nicer.' The slogan captures the incoherence of modern anti-capitalism. It is clear what the demonstrators are against, but not clear what they are for.'[13] For most people living ordinary lives in Europe and the United States, to be described as a capitalist might be unwelcome, to fight for the ideological idea of capitalism might be unthinkable, but whether it be called freedom, free market or even social democracy, the tenets of capitalism are in our bones and way of life.

Average Joe

During the 2008 Presidential campaign in the United States, Samuel Joseph Wurzelbacher, a plumber from Ohio, became known to households across the world. 'Joe the Plumber' as he is better known was a small businessman whose chance encounter with Democrat nominee Barak Obama made headline news. Joe questioned Obama's tax plans and in doing so was catapulted into the campaign. Republican John McCain repeatedly used 'Joe the Plumber' as the archetypal American, put upon by the state.

The Average Joe in the United States just like the 'Average Pepe' in Europe is worthy of a little attention. According to the US Census Bureau, in 2005 the median personal income for those earning was $28,567. To put this into a broader perspective their figures published in 2009, showed real median household income in the United States in 2008 was a little over $50,000 (down 3.6% on the year). Beneath this number there was substantial disparity with white households at $55,000 (down 2.6%) and Hispanics at just under $38,000 (down 5.6%). Beyond this, the distribution of earnings by race, sex, geography, education and pretty much any other measure was far from equal. Indeed, income inequality had a Gini coefficient of 0.466 (a measure of inequality where 0 is perfectly equal and 1 is perfectly unequal)[14]. By way of a quick and dirty comparison, median gross annual earnings in the UK were just under £21,000 (up 2.6%) in 2008-9 with earnings of £59,000 pulling one into the top 5%[15]. And on the Gini Index Germany scores 0.27, France 0.33, the UK 0.34 and the EU as a whole 0.31.[16]

Earnings helped consumerism flourish and the average American or Western European is now able to own their own home, go on vacation and drive a car. King of the automobiles, there are a staggering 765 motor vehicles in the United States per 1000 people representing the most in the world; 566 in

Italy, 471 in Spain, 426 in the UK. Nigeria and Madagascar average at a sorry 1 per 1000.[17] In their own way the cars in Madagascar and the USA are each tragedies of our riches.

To bring home the bacon though, we have to put in the work. The average American works around 1777 hours per year, the average Briton 1652, German 1362 and French worker 1346 and in the Netherlands 1309.[18] The trend in Europe being curtailed in recent years by the Working Time Directive, but still representing a sizeable portion of one's life. Aguiar and Hunt's study of leisure over five decades suggests that leisure for American men has nonetheless increased by 6-9 hours per week since the 1960s and 4-8 hours for women but 'document a growing inequality in leisure that is the mirror image of the growing inequality of wages and expenditures.'[19]

Average Joe is a postmodern being, emerging as a contemporary incarnation amid advanced capitalism. Attitudes and values are steeped in consumerism, pluralism, technology, globalisation and individualism.[20] The World Values Survey has been running since 1981 and analysis has suggested profound changes in attitudes. It shows that as countries become wealthier, they become happier, except in industrialised, rich economies where there is no relationship between income and wellbeing.

Ronald Inglehart's analysis of this too discovered significant differences in the values expressed by younger and older generations. 'Among the oldest age groups, we found an overwhelming majority to be materialists; those who gave top priority to economic and physical security outnumbered the post-materialists (those who gave top priority to belonging and self-expression) by fourteen to one. But as we move from older to younger groups, the proportion of materialists declines and the proportion of post-materialists increases. Among the postwar generation, post-materialists outnumber materialists.'[21] It suggests either that we become more materialistic as we age (or as we accumulate wealth) or that the generation which is most materialistic today – the baby boomers who are central to this story – have always been the most acquisitive. The irony is that many of us do not want to live like this; we are not even sure that we want the material possessions.

The Harwood Group's survey of American attitudes reported that people 'want to have financial security and live in material comfort, but their deepest aspirations are non-material ones. People also struggle to reconcile their condemnation of other Americans' choices on consumption with their core belief in the freedom to live as we choose. Thus, while people may want to act on their concerns, they are paralyzed by the tensions and contradictions embedded in their own beliefs. In turn, they shy away from examining too closely not only their own behavior, but that of others.'[22]

But Average Josephine spends very easily and as a collective is extraordinary. $12 billion dollars is spent annually by Europeans and Americans on perfume. That is about the same amount as the GDP of Jamaica just on smelling nice. American's alone spend $8 billion a year on cosmetics[23] and Eric Schlosser's *Fast Food Nation* reported that some $110billion was spent on burgers, fries, pizzas and the rest in the USA during 2000.[24] In recession hit 2008, the average Italian spent more than €1200 on clothes and shoes.[25] In fashionable London, it is not uncommon to find £40 being spent a time on blow drying hair. We know how to spend.

Average is difficult to define but even a cursory glance over the numbers shows a great deal of conformity and constraint in the way that lives are lived. Earnings are relatively high but the average number disguises considerable disparity in the dispersion of income. We are apt to consume but even growing leisure time is hardly the freedom we might promise ourselves.

In true American showbiz style, 'Average Joe' Wurzelbacher found fame, appearing in television commercials, publishing a book (*Joe the Plumber: fighting for the American dream*), becoming a motivational speaker, and even a commentator who, improbably, was found reporting from Israel on the conflict in the Middle East.

What Did We Think We Would Get?

Did we always expect our world and our lives to develop and be shaped in this way? Was this the grand plan for the capitalism and policymaking which our societies and our politicians promoted? It might not have been a bad objective if it had. After all, Western lives are comfortable and on the whole safe. We have created (and one might argue destroyed) more wealth than the world has ever seen. We consume in vast quantities, access cheap and efficient travel and own a huge amount of material possessions. And our politics are generally open and democratic. But somehow it was all meant to be better than this.

In those tense yet optimistic years following the Second World War, futurology was in abundance. It had never really gone away and those same images of Fritz Lang's 1927 futuristic film *Metropolis* survived into the 1950s and 1960s: great urban cities in the sky inhabited by robots, with roads in the firmament intertwined with personal flying machines. For most who predicted life in the twenty first century from the comfort in the fifties, technology was the greatest, and perhaps most trivial, source of inspiration. Flying cars, space travel and instant food were among the most popular predictions and in their own way reflected the era. There were little of the social tensions of capitalism which epitomises Lang's dystopia, produced as it was during the Weimar Republic. In this new era, people worried about a third world war, this time with the communist Soviet Union, and the ability of agriculture to feed the population and they looked to the moon on which man would soon step. These fears and hope found their way into many visions of the future. But what of the rest?

'*How Experts Think We'll Live in 2000 AD*' was the exciting title of a 1950 Associated Press symposium featuring several AP specialists. Replete with a striking montage of a scientist before brutal modernist buildings, rocket ships, and a relaxed pipe smoker, it confidently foretold our destiny. We would have a man made planet circling the earth, industrial and agricultural production would be able to support 300 million, 'a housewife may use an electronic stove and prepare roast beef in less time than it takes to set the table', women will be six feet tall taking a size eleven shoe 'have shoulders like a wrestler and muscles like a truck driver'. 'She will be doing a man's job' and might even be President. There was no mention though of civil rights for blacks or broader issues of equality. Elsewhere, it saw medical advances, improved public health, and 'foolproof flying'. Predicting that civilian aviation 'will be accepted by the public as readily as mid-century's automobile and train… we shall be neighbors of everyone else on earth,' it nonetheless foresaw none of the harsh reality of an interdependent world we would come to experience.

Perhaps more prophetically, of politics it reported that 'some see us drifting toward the all-powerful state, lulled by the sweet sound of "security". Some see a need to curb our freedom lest it be used to shield those who plot against us.' More optimistically though, 'there will be more graduates of colleges than there are high school graduates today.' And 'by the end of the century many government plans now avoided as forms of socialism will be accepted as commonplace. Who in 1900 thought that by mid-century there would be government regulated pensions and a work week limited to 40 hours? A minimum wage, child labor curbs and unemployment compensation? So tell your children not to be surprised if the year 2000 finds a 35 or even a 20 hour week fixed by law.'[26]

Others too, such as the innovative pollster Bud Lewis, believed that technology would all but replace work telling a 1966 radio audience that 'we're going to have to readjust our old, puritan perhaps, concepts of what a person should de with his life... there's not going to be all the jobs there used to be around.'[27] Ignorant of the economics of industrialisation or what we now know about deindustrialisation perhaps (see chapter 8), there was nonetheless a widely held vision of 'large incomes and short work weeks... people will have devoted adequate portions of their incomes to overcome successfully water and air pollution, congested roads and airways, and many disease, both physical and social.' This according to Richard Gillis Jr. in 1969 who also told his audience that they 'should work for an educational system that will enlarge man's understanding, control and enjoyment of life.'[28]

It seems that the future we now inhabit was never intended to make us the richest peoples who had ever lived in terms of our ability to consume and work harder and longer for the privilege. The future was meant to give us more control, more leisure, more peace, longer active lives, and more happiness.

John F. Kennedy

If ever there were a political leader who came to embody the idea of optimism of the future it was JFK, America's most glamorous and (after Teddy Roosevelt) youngest, President. Kennedy represented change. He represented a change in generation in the White House as much as he represented a change in sentiment from the old order of the Second World War and great depression. That his background was rich and privileged did not prevent him from appealing to ordinary voters. That to be a Kennedy was to be part of the establishment did not prevent him from offering himself as something fresh and new. His inaugural address, as famous as of any President before or since, summoned up an optimism of what could be achieved in the 1960s and beyond.

The world is very different now. For man holds in his mortal hands the power to abolish all forms of human poverty and all forms of human life. And yet the same revolutionary beliefs for which our forebears fought are still at issue around the globe - the belief that the rights of man come not from the generosity of the state but from the hand of God...

Now the trumpet summons us again - not as a call to bear arms, though arms we need - not as a call to battle, though embattled we are - but a call to bear the burden of a long twilight struggle, year in and year out, 'rejoicing in hope, patient in tribulation' - a struggle against the common enemies of man: tyranny, poverty, disease and war itself...

In the long history of the world, only a few generations have been granted the role of defending freedom in its hour of maximum danger. I do not shrink from this responsibility - I welcome it. I do not believe that any of us would exchange places with any other people or any other generation. The energy, the faith, the devotion which we bring to this endeavour will light our country and all who serve it - and the glow from that fire can truly light the world.[29]

The speech and the presidency embodied the very balance between hope and fear that the early postwar generation had come to live under. This was all the more so in America, still finding its feet as a superpower and as one side of an ideological battle that figures like Kennedy assured Americans that it could and would win. With his presidency cut short, Kennedy would never have to answer just why his administration achieved (historically at least) very little. His successors, Johnson and Nixon went on to see civil rights reform and the lunar space programme respectively and yet it is JFK, still the most popular of Presidents, who reaps the credit (and tends not to be blamed for Vietnam). Good looking, charismatic and a great communicator, Kennedy was the first President of the television age. The presidential campaign with that first candidates' debate, the inauguration, Marilyn Monroe singing 'Happy Birthday' and finally his assassination all took place on the small screen and became the first of our great television events.

Intriguingly as a younger man, Kennedy struggled with public speaking and his long term health issues meant that he was not the fit and energetic young man portrayed. His personal qualities too are left wanting in a comparison to say a Bill Clinton or a Ronald Reagan. They each fought their way to the top with great self-belief. JFK in this sense is privileged and somewhat overshadowed, as a young man, by his ancestors: his grandfather 'Honey' Fitz, an immigrant who achieved money and power in Boston, and his father Joe Kennedy a businessman, banker and political figure whose ambition it was that his eldest son would become President. That son was Joseph Kennedy Jnr, killed in England during the Second World War. The mantle fell to John.

It did not matter it seems because JFK began what is today's personality politics; where perceived character and image are what matters. And for the story of these pages, Kennedy has a special place. By holding the unattractive record of the shortest lived of any US President, assassinated in Dallas at the age of just 46, it means that for the generation inspired by his rhetoric JFK is forever young. He would never be an old remote figure or a president shamed by his record. Forever, Kennedy represents hope for a future that perhaps never was.

Legacy for the Second Decaders

The second decaders have experienced a somewhat limited destiny which has become focused on the creation and maintenance of our riches. Many people would now see that this is far more parochial than that which an advanced society should offer or seek to achieve. Perhaps, during the two decades since the Berlin Wall fell and the West believed itself to be the world's ideological victor, we have forgotten why we wanted the riches or indeed lost sight of our priorities today. Prosperity was surely central to the utopia but it has become the ends rather than the means raising questions about self-interest being to our own detriment. We have not fulfilled the optimistic visions of a better world which the futurologists of the 1950s and 1960s foresaw. Visions which were, after all, capitalist in formation centred on freedom, security, democracy, health and wellbeing. What we have become is rich.

Chapter Two

The Origins of Our Riches

Despite the depressing and somewhat frightening economic backdrop, there was a tangible air of excitement in Gordon Brown's London. It is April 2009 and, accompanied by a five hundred strong entourage of aides, guards, doctors and chefs, several decoy helicopters and a tear gas launching, titanium constructed limousine, known simply as 'the beast', Barak Obama is making his first visit to Britain as President of the United States. Obama was the new superstar everyone wanted to see and be seen with. By his election, it seemed, he had single handily renewed America's flagging reputation in the world.

Gone was the divisive, blunt and incoherent George Bush; here was an elegant and articulate President in which Europe and the world could finally believe. But this was more than a vanity exercise for world leaders hoping some of that glamour would rub off on them. This visit was more important than usual for this was the G20 meeting of industrialised nations and their task was to stabilise a world economy which had come close to meltdown. The collapse of the international investment bank Lehman Brothers and the accompanying banking bailout the previous September had perhaps been the nadir of the economic crisis. But it was far from the end. The following months had seen the world descend into the worst recession since the 1930s. And there was a very real fear that the 2010s would become a new great depression. There was a real fear that our great riches, the wealth and lifestyles we take for granted, was under the greatest threat since Hitler's war.

The world responded in London that April. With uncharacteristic unity, the meeting drew to a close with an agreement to inject a staggering $1.1 trillion into the global economy. Obama heralded the London summit as 'historic. It was historic because of the size and the scope of the challenges that we face, and because of the timeliness and magnitude of our response.' He added: 'You know, it's hard for 20 heads of state to bridge their differences. We've all got our own national policies; we all have our own assumptions, our own political cultures. But our citizens are all hurting. They all need us to come together'.[1] While some saw this as notable for its constructive international co-operation, others were shocked at the sheer size of the funds these rich nations were able to muster and commit to fiscal stimulus and rescue over the space of just a few hours (and considerable pre-summit negotiations).

Oxfam compared the sums conjured to save the banks with the relatively modest amount required to tackle world poverty. 'The $8.42 trillion promised by rich country governments to bailout banks would be enough to end global extreme poverty for 50 years and a massive step towards ending it forever… leaders could make a massive difference to the world's poorest people by diverting a tiny fraction of the bailout money to provide an economic stimulus, social safety nets and health services for those affected by the economic crisis.'[2]

In one fell swoop the summit contrasted the riches of the developed (and parts of the developing) world with the poverty of the millions who comprise the poorest people on the planet. The story is not simply one of a crisis in global capitalism, it is one which, in huge green dollar symbols, demonstrates the great success of capitalism in creating such massive wealth since the Second World War. The scale of the riches we had amassed over those decades was there for us all to see and that 'hurting' which the President described was the hurting of the very fortunate. Paul Krugman's chillingly realistic description epitomises our fortunate lives:

> *The world is an unfair place. Wealthy countries tend to be blessed on all counts. Not only are they rich but they generally have stable and effective governments. And they fall on the good side of the double standard: investors and markets tend to give them the benefit of the doubt. All this gives them a freedom of action, an ability to cope with economic problems that poorer nations can only envy.*[3]

In the West we have rarely been richer. In contrast to billions of people living in the emerging economies of the world, ordinary Britons, Germans, French, Americans, Canadians and Australians no longer have to worry about being able to eat, put shelter over their heads or heat their homes. For those at the bottom of society, life is surely difficult, and in a downturn it hurts more than usual, but in the West we are lucky; the downside is limited. We perhaps forget this. The Young Foundation published a fascinating account which examined 'who was sinking and who was swimming' in contemporary Britain. It is a report that this book will return to later in this chapter when considering inequality and in a subsequent chapter which explores wellbeing since raw economic power tells only a small fragment of the story. Nevertheless, their comprehensive study of 'need', from food to housing to warmth to transport to possessions and activities to skills as well as numerous other measures showed concerning levels of unmet need, especially when compared to other countries in Europe. But the absolute levels of poverty remain low in what is a rich society; a fact which creates its own serious problems and will also be returned to. And as the report points out, 'policy is often concerned with what some consider to be fairly arbitrary numbers, such as the definition of poverty as below 60% of average incomes, a definition which is both unknown by the great majority of the public and not intuitively obvious either'.[4] So what does this mean for our riches?

In a dated though still relevant study, Rosenberg and Birdzell argue that pluralism was as important as technological advancement in our economic development but also demonstrate that by almost any comparative measure, today we in the West are fortunate to be wealthy. They open their book, *How the West Grew Rich*, with the bold statement that:

> *If we take the long view of history and judge the economic lives of our ancestors by modern standards, it is a story of almost unrivalled wretchedness. The typical human society has given only a small number of people a humane existence, while the great majority have lived in abysmal squalor. We are led to forget the domineering mystery of other times… remembered as golden eras of pastoral simplicity. They were not.*[5]

A comparison of our comfortable lives today with those of our great-great grandparents demonstrates the riches we now enjoy. Destitute Europeans left for the new world amid starvation, disease and persecution not so long ago. Their world was very different from our rich lives today. The very same observation can be made by comparing the great global world of the twenty-first century; those riches we enjoy and the squalor suffered by millions. A few thousand miles and we could step back a few hundred years in economic terms. Indeed, it is our riches that are unusual not the deprivation elsewhere. Those of us who live in the developed world exist in a bubble separated by a short journey in time and a shorter one in geography. And it is these very same abnormal circumstances which have fuelled the belief (and indeed sometimes the reality) in the American Dream of riches and success obtainable by anyone. But it is a belief which Alex Brassey argues 'points to a more pernicious, self-destructive force, a force in which the drive to succeed, to reach the dream is filled with the need to pursue ever more ambitious targets, fuelled by ever larger desires which can never and will never be fulfilled.'[6] The reality of the American Dream is the reality of the Young Foundation Survey in Britain; it ignores the blocks to social mobility. Yet it remains powerful since it 'puts an emphasis on economic growth, personal wealth and independence.'[7] And by any objective measure it highlights how rich America and Europe really are.

The Past is Another Country - How Rich Are We?

Our bubble separates us from the squalor of the recent past and the want of the majority of the earth's growing population. If you are reading this book, the chances are you are one of the richest people alive today or indeed one of the richest people who have ever lived. A person with post-tax income of $20,000 per year is in the wealthiest 4.6% of the world's six billion strong, inhabitants, earning some eighteen times more than that of the 'typical person'. To get into the top one percent, one only has to earn $38,500 after tax.[8] We perhaps forget how rich we are in the comfortable West with our cosy and safe housing stuffed full of electrical equipment and consumer goods, clean sanitation, power on demand, protein aplenty, cars, education, health, and the freedoms of civilization. In part this is because of wealth relativity; we relate to those around us, identify, increasingly, with celebrities and do not make the connection with those across the world who survive on a fraction of our disposable incomes.

A plethora of websites have emerged showing us just how wealthy we are on a global scale. They are fun, appalling and revealing. A modestly paid university academic for instance might find himself as the 44 millionth richest person in the world, falling into the top 0.74% of the global population.[9] And yet he might not consider himself to be rich. If one is lucky enough to be in the top 5% or so of world earners, wealth relativity works in two directions: relative to the richest in society and relative to the poorest. But, being based on one's own society, the downside is limited and all too tangible while the upside is galloping away at an unmatchable speed. The wealth proportions evidenced across the globe reappear in our own world. In the United States, for instance, some 85% of the wealth is controlled by the richest 20% of the population; the richest 1% of Americans own almost 35%. This means that the vast majority of Americans, around 243 million ordinary people, share just 15% of the country's net worth between them. The figures become more polarised if one deducts the property value of the principal residence and it is notable that the gap has continued to grow over recent decades, helped along its way with a generous dose of Reaganomics in the 1980s.[10] Stephen Haseler has described the growth of the super-rich (and 'mega-rich'), who distinguish themselves from 'ordinary millionaires', living in gated communities, an overclass separated from the constraints of countries. 'Get the world's top 3 mega-rich (dollar billionaires) people into one room at the turn of the century and you would have assembled command over more resources than the GNP of Israel,'[11] he tells us, '....Intriguingly, the super-rich hold their wealth in very different ways from average middle-income households.... In 2006 [they] invested 31 per cent of their financial assets in equities, 24 per cent in real estate.'[12] And if it is not this mega-rich elite with whom we identify and compare ourselves then it is certainly the 'ordinary millionaires' we see in our own societies and on our televisions each and every day. Rarely will our wealth relativity encompass the starving of Africa.

A case in point is Fidelity's 2011 survey of American millionaires. The research questioned those with investable assets of at least $1 million but where the survey average was $3.5 million. It found that a whole 42% reported that they did not feel wealthy and to 'feel rich' respondents needed at least $7.5 million.[13]

And yet if we were to compare our riches with those of Africa and the poorest corners of the world, our wealth is put into perspective. The European Union today (enlarged to include the poorer nations of the East) had a 2009 GDP per capita (Purchasing Power Parity) of a little under 30,000 International Dollars compared with the more exclusive G7 at almost $39,000; Sub-Saharan Africa by contrast reaches little over $2,000.[14] One might imagine this gulf has always existed. Alas it has not. In his study of global poverty, the celebrated economist Jeffrey Sachs points out that in the early nineteenth century, average incomes in Europe and Africa and other parts of the world were broadly the same, as was life expectancy (at about 40 years). In those two centuries to follow, however, global wealth grew at a phenomenal pace and it was concentrated on what are today the most industrialised economies of the world. And significantly, it was not that this growth was fast (as China's has been in recent years for instance) but rather that it was consistent.[15] This means that today we are separated from the poverty of the past and of the present, and for the most part remain blissfully ignorant.

In his December 2009 Pre-Budget Report, the then British Chancellor of the Exchequer, Alistair Darling (salary £144,520,[16] 0.001% of the richest people on earth, 107.5 millionth richest) imposed a one-off windfall tax of 50% (plus the standard 40% making an effective charge of 70%) on bankers' bonuses in excess of £25,000. It was felt that profits substantially subsidised by the taxpayer should not be paid in such large sums to a section of society who bore considerable blame for the financial crisis which began in 2008. While those on lower salaries were paying the price of economic intervention which prevented banking meltdown, the recipients of this huge state aid, the banks, all but appeared to have returned to 'business as usual'. It led Bank of England Governor Mervyn King (salary £283,564,[17] same richest ranking as the Chancellor) to make a rather waspish speech:

'To paraphrase a great wartime leader,' he told his audience, 'never in the field of financial endeavour has so much money been owed by so few to so many - and, one might add, so far with little real reform.'[18] The intervention coincided with statistics from the Centre for Economics and Business Research that revealed a 50% annual rise in City bonuses from £4bn to £6bn.[19] What is perhaps more intriguing is that a £25,000 bonus alone would put the recipient in the top 1.42% of earners or the 85.5m richest person on the planet. Alas, the chorus of dissent from the banking community (individuals on the whole rather than institutions) led many of the banks to absorb the tax themselves ironically increasing the Treasury's take. Bankers, who by then had become just about the most vilified group of people on the planet for their central role in causing the credit crunch, displayed a lack of contrition or even sensitivity. Theirs was a sense of entitlement; a sense that they had worked hard (which undoubtedly many had done) and deserved this money, which for most recipients meant multiples of Darling's minimum. Their, not so idle, threat was that they would depart these shores for more sympathetic tax regimes (though not necessarily governments willing to underwrite their errors) overseas. The hubris which surrounded these most highly paid of people extended to a widely reported interview Goldman Sachs Chairman and CEO, Lloyd Blankfein gave to the London Sunday Times:

> *'I know I could slit my wrists and people would cheer,' he says. But then, he slowly begins to argue the case for modern banking. 'We're very important,' he says, abandoning self-flagellation. 'We help companies to grow by helping them to raise capital. Companies that*

grow create wealth. This, in turn, allows people to have jobs that create more growth and more wealth. It's a virtuous cycle.' To drive home his point, he makes a remarkably bold claim. 'We have a social purpose.'[20]

But it was a concluding remark which received the most attention telling his interviewer that he was 'doing God's work'. There have always been the disproportionately wealthy and disproportionately powerful but in our rich and democratic societies even the poorest find it easier to identify with the mega rich than with anyone from outside of the bubble. The truth of this episode is, however, that we have lost touch with the usual state of man and we have done so in a single generation.

The Selfish Generation

The lives of the baby boomers, those born in Europe and the United States in the aftermath of the Second World War, have on the whole been ones of great fortune. Indeed in stark contrast to their parents and one could argue their children, the seventy six million Americans and similar numbers of Europeans born between the end of the war and the beginning of the swinging sixties have enjoyed almost unprecedented economic prosperity, shelter, sustenance, welfare, education, employment, disposable income, consumer products, foreign travel, early retirement, pensions and life expectancy.[21] For the most part, their lives have been comfortable. They have enjoyed a quality of life paid for by their parents in blood and their children in arrears. Some sixty million soldiers and civilians died as a result of the Second World War; many others were injured or left homeless. Churchill's summing up of 'their finest hour', was less about the fighting and violence of conflict than a generation which accepted the price of freedom for their children as being 'whatever the cost may be'. The contrast is stark. The American journalist and self-appointed spokesman for the generation of baby boomer offspring, Anya Kamenetz, reported that in a survey that asked baby boomers if they would sacrifice their own economic wellbeing for their children, the majority said 'no'. 'We have all come of age of part of generation debt,' she argues.[22] Indeed, the parents of the baby boomers had endured the double whammy of depression and then war, both of which delayed marriage and the starting of families. This is a critique which is even finding favour on the so called centre right. The British Conservative politician, David Willetts, a man widely known as 'two brains' on account of his intelligent contributions to public policy thinking, published a 2010 book entitled *The Pinch: how the baby boomers took their children's future and why they should give it back*. A provocative book, especially so coming from a prominent Conservative, Willets makes the case that we suffer from generational inequalities as the baby boomers have accumulated a disproportionate share of the wealth and exercise disproportional demographic power. They have failed to pass on opportunities to their children's generation.[23]

In mitigation, the baby boomers maintained peace in Europe, promoted cultural harmony, extended the arts and invented our modern technology.

But the baby boomers have been the most selfish generation in contemporary history. This is the generation which consumed natural resources at a pace not seen before, stomping across the world leaving size twelve carbon footprints in their tracks. It was the generation which enjoyed free education, had too few children themselves and which demands lower taxes. Theirs has been a life of consumption and to this day cause the greatest environmental damage. A report in 2007 from the University of York showed that the baby boomers have the highest carbon footprint of all generations which, at 13.52 tonnes per capita per year, is as much as 10%-20% higher than any other age group.[24] And as they age, such is the consumptive power of this generation that an equity index (MLFOY) has been created to track companies offering healthcare services to these boomers.

They were the disposable generation. The generation for whom as rationing came to an end 'mend and make do' would never be a mantra. The demand for new things: new housing, new furniture, new kitchens, new clothes, new cars all paid for on easy credit.

They are at the centre of a story in which we are all characters. They were born into the world which became that which we recognise today; one which in the aftermath of world war came to prioritise the creation and maintenance of wealth, in its broadest sense, over all other policy objectives. They were the generation which 'won' the greatest ideological debate the world has ever seen. They were the generation who ultimately limited the vision for what politics can and should do and limited the destiny of the second decaders. And it is the legacy of that generation which shapes the way we live our lives today.

Depression and the Golden Age of Capitalism

The riches enjoyed by the developed West did not surface after 1945. There is a long history dating back centuries to exploration, imperialism, trade and industrialisation. There is also an historical ideological commitment to capitalism just as Marxism flourished in revolutionary Russia. Even the likes of the Frankfurt school, which emerged during the inter-war period, distanced intellectual thought from the popular interpretation of Marx's writings. The eighteenth and nineteenth centuries were important for the economic growth of today's industrialised economies and these years distinguish our riches from the poorest parts of the planet. But in contrast to the everyday squalor, the hard lives experienced by much of the population over the years before 1945, when some made their fortunes while others struggled to survive, the post-war Western world has been about capitalism, economic growth and riches for all. The children of the baby boomers grew up in the strife-ridden 1970s and the fractious 1980s which eventually celebrated the excesses of individualism. But for those whose early life occurred in the decades after the war, life was simple, but on the whole rather good. The Second World War had brought to an end a decade of squalor that was the great depression. During the 1930s, capitalism had all but failed. The 1929 Wall Street crash brought an end to the excess of the roaring twenties to usher in unemployment, economic retrenchment, degradation and want.

For the wealthy minority those years might well have been a seamless continuation of the excessive 1920s but for the rest, life was hard. Nevertheless we must avoid too harsh caricatures of the period as Stevenson and Cook remind us:

For those in work, the 1930s were a period of rising living standards and new levels of consumption... This was a paradox which lay at the heart of Britain in the thirties, where new levels of prosperity contrasted with the intractable problems of mass unemployment and the depressed areas.[25]

In the autumn of 1932, as many as three thousand people marched from the north of England, the Welsh valleys and Glasgow to London's Hyde Park as part of a great hunger march. Unemployment in some regions had been a devastating 70%. Food was scarce, shelter poor and access to health care limited. Nigel Gray's captivating oral history of the depression features the Londoner Gladys Gibson whose fascinating reflections are a reminder that a passing generation knew a different country and a different world from ours:

Many of the undernourished unemployed had ulcers or incipient ulcers, as you could see from their drawn faces...[26]

The effects of long unemployment were terrible. Men on the scrap heap became cynical, aggressive or hopeless. The hard thing was to persuade them they were not 'done for'. A lot depended on the attitude of the family. The man had lost his position as chief wage earner and young people resented having their earnings taken into account by The Board. Many left home. One man of sixty, with a family of adolescents, drew just five Shillings.[27]

The story was similar across Europe. In William Shirer's chilling account of the rise of the Third Reich the disastrous disintegration of German exports and subsequent scarcity of imported essentials following the Wall Street crash represented not only hardship for German people but also an opportunity which Hitler would not ignore.

The misery of the German people, their lives still scarred by the disastrous collapse of the Mark less than ten years before, did not arouse his compassion. On the contrary, in the darkest days of the period, when the factories were silent, when the registered unemployed numbered over six million and bread lines stretched for blocks in every city in the land, he could write in the Nazi press: 'Never in my life have I been so well disposed and inwardly contented as in these days.'[28]

And what more vivid an image of the period can there be than Hooverville? These shanty towns which appeared across the United States and most prominently in New York's Central Park, housed thousands of newly homeless Americans in tents and rickety, makeshift shelters.

The shanty towns simultaneously attracted admiration and censure: people admired the resourcefulness of the individual inhabitants and the extent of their efforts and yet were threatened by the implicit disorder of such colonies. Government could seem benign but also cruel. When the East River colony was cleared in 1933 (with 10 days' notice) "old John Cahill" told a reporter: "Nobody's askin' us where we're goin'. There's not a soul thinkin' about us."[29]

As Europe and the United States turned to a new peace in 1945, the vast industrial production which had been developed to process the bloodiness of war was converted into peaceful aims of reconstruction, manufacturing and export. Capitalism had finally redeemed itself and the 1950s and 1960s provided an economic comfort and prosperity lost to those who endured the slump. The golden age of capitalism[30] was a period of Western economic expansion which provided the foundations of our riches today.

For proponents of John Maynard Keynes, the architect of post war economic policies, the period compares favourably not only to the dire days of the depression but also to the free market Reaganomics of more recent decades. The golden age, according to Robert Skidelsky, for instance saw global growth at an annual average of 4.8% compared to 3.2% during the 'Washington Consensus' years with US unemployment averaging 4.8% compared to 6.1%. Unemployment in Europe is even starker. In France, the golden age saw a fall to 1.2% compared to 9.5% since; Germany 3.1% compared to 7.5%.[31]

British prime minister, Harold Macmillan's 1957 proclamation that 'most of our people have never had it so good' rings true to this day and it helped him secure victory at the 1959 general election. Britain enjoyed economic growth, prosperity and an average annual unemployment rate as low 1.6% between 1950-69. Memories did not have to be too long to recall the 20% unemployment experienced by the end of 1930.

These were the economic boom years which coincided with new fashions, technology, American culture and rebellious music. By the end of the golden age, which must be considered to be something like the oil crisis of 1973, a man had even walked on the moon. The golden age created our modern societies which had wealth, consumerism and consumption at their heart. There were tougher times too. During the 1970s, Western capitalism seemed in decline and then during 1980s there was economic strife, unemployment and fractious societies. But in the long run living standards continued to improve. GDP per capita between 1973 and 1998 increased from $16,689 (1990 international dollars) to $27331 in the United States ($23,214 by 1990); $12,022 to $18714 in the United Kingdom; $11,966 to $17,799 in Germany; $11,439 to $20413 in Japan. By comparison, African GDP per capita rose from $1,365 to $1,368; the world as a whole $4,104 to $5,709 over the period.[32] Other indicators such as life expectancy and height tell a similar story. For the baby boomers enduring their first real economic slowdown, the 1970s was a period where property was purchased at historically low prices and where a bout of inflation was to erode the debt upon which it was secured. It is for this reason that the baby boomers did rather well out of post war capitalism and why, as their generation begins retirement, even a global economic downturn on the scale of that experienced after 2008, has not led to a fundamental rethink over the place of our riches as perhaps it did in the 1930s.

Huey P. Long

In the tradition of Americans assassinating their most popular of politicians, Huey Long was shot dead in 1935 at the age of 42.[33] This Louisiana Governor and then Senator became a radical figure during the early years of the great depression, promoting ideas which would astonish modern day observers. When, as Governor in 1929, he proposed a five percent tax on oil production to pay for social programmes, there was an attempt to impeach him leading to a brawl in the State Legislature. Throughout his career he used a mix of popular democracy and strong- arm tactics to fight his opponents, including firing them and their relatives from government jobs, founding his own local newspaper to counter journalistic opposition and running as senator by way of a referendum on proposals defeated in the State.

Opposing Roosevelt's New Deal on the grounds of inadequacy, Long unveiled his 'Share Our Wealth' plan which argued that lack of wealth was not America's problem but rather its concentration. He told his radio audience in 1935:

> *It became apparent that the billionaires and multimillionaires even began to squeeze out the common millionaires, closing in and taking their properties and wrecking their businesses. And so we arrived (and are still there) at the place that in abundant America where we have everything for which a human heart can pray, the hundreds of millions-or, as General Johnson says, the 80 million-of our people are crying in misery for the want of the things which they need for life, notwithstanding the fact that the country has had and can have more than the entire human race can consume.*[34]

He proposed radical redistribution by way of progressive taxation on wealth which kicked in after the first million dollars at a reasonable one percent but reached one hundred percent after nine million as was income over a million dollars. He was, consequently, a divisive figure. When in 1933 he drunkenly urinated on the shoe of an unsuspecting member of the Sands Point Club he received a bloody punch in the face in retaliation. The magazine *Collier's Weekly* raised $1000 from its readers to make a gold medal to be awarded to the unknown assailant.

The Rich Underclass

And so today, in Europe, the United States and other parts of the developed world, we enjoy great wealth. Average incomes are vast by comparison to the poorest countries in the world and even those struggling to get by on the most meagre of earnings in no way compare to the want which scars the Earth. The World Bank provides some definitions of poverty using referencing lines of living on between $1.25 and $2 per day (2005 PPP). Their estimates suggest something in the region of 1.4 billion people were living on less than the lower level in 2005.[35] Such absolute poverty limits not only life chances but limits life itself. It means very real hunger, disease and minimal shelter; education and healthcare are absent along with power and political freedoms so easily taken for granted in the West.

When we talk of poverty in our rich societies we mean something very different. Relative poverty is less about starvation than about inequality. If one uses the EU's definition of living below 60% of an economy's mean earnings, some strange results surface. A rather intriguing story emerged in 2009 when the European Commission reported that the UK had the fourth highest level of poverty in the EU for the over 65s with approaching a third of pensioners living in 'poverty'; there was the UK categorised alongside much poorer countries such as Lithuania and below Romania. It was all the more intriguing because counter statistics from the Department of Work and Pensions showed that not only were incomes for these people considerably higher than their counterparts who ranked above them in the list but also that pensioner income was 10% above EU average.[36] The reality was not that their incomes were lower but rather that they fell below a fairly arbitrary line relative to the wealth of their own societies. A handful of Russian Oligarchs immigrate with enough Roubles to buy a chunk of Chelsea and British relative poverty increases; a stockmarket crash reduces portfolio valuations of the super rich, and a few people are dragged out of poverty all without a penny of difference to actual incomes of those at the bottom. As such, some would argue that it simply does not matter. They would agree with Margaret Thatcher who, during a 1975 speech in the USA, claimed:

The pursuit of equality itself is a mirage. Opportunity means nothing unless it includes the right to be unequal and of freedom to be different. One of the reasons why we value individuals is not because they're all the same but because they're different... Let our children grow tall and some taller than others, if they have the ability in them to do so.[37]

Such meritocracy which weaved its way into policy during and after the 1980s has created great wealth as we have seen. But great riches have not created great societies. Indeed, as Wilkinson and Pickett state in their incredible book, *The Spirit*

Level, 'modern societies are, despite their affluence, social failures.'[38] The book, far from a polemic, draws on extensive data to demonstrate that average income is irrelevant to overall wellbeing but rather it is the difference between the richest and the poorest in a given society which matters. 'The problems in rich countries are not caused by the society not being rich enough (or being too rich) but by the scale of material differences between people in each society being too big.'[39]

The jaw dropping results conclude that, once a country becomes 'rich', further increases in average wealth will not make any difference to important measures such as life expectancy. Indeed, they show that a country can be twice as rich as another and the poorer of the two can perform better, in terms of citizens' wellbeing, if it is more equal. That Young Foundation report concerned with those at the very bottom of society produced complementary results. Warning that vulnerable groups have different needs and that we learn more by analysing separately, they nonetheless show that for many in this underclass, life lacks meaning and that this group is wider than simply the very poorest. 'Most past definitions of this group right at the bottom have focussed on material needs... [but the analysis] gives us a picture of the people who are least connected to human love, care and warmth.'[40] This is indeed a tragedy of our riches.

In a very real sense our societies protect wealth and the wealthy. Reiman and Leighton's controversial and frequently re-printed account argues that many of the most harmful things to us in the workplace, in the medical profession, in the environment and elsewhere are simply not criminal (but perhaps ought to be). The criminal justice system, they argue, 'is a carnival mirror that presents a distorted image of what threatens us.'[41] The consequence, according to their thesis, is a system which perpetuates the very societies about which *The Spirit Level* warns us:

> *In our view it comes as no surprise that our prisons and jails predominantly confine the poor. This is not because these are the individuals who most threaten us. It is because the criminal justice system effectively weeds out the well-to-do.... The image of the criminal population one sees in our [United States] nation's jails and prisons is distorted by the shape of the criminal justice system itself.*[42]

The poorest in our societies, therefore, represent a rich underclass by international standards. They will not usually starve, lack access to healthcare or find themselves politically disenfranchised. For 'the vast majority of people in affluent countries the difficulties of life are no longer about filling our stomachs, having clean water and keeping warm. Most of us wish we could eat less rather than more.'[43] The great 'underclass issues' are issues of disengagement from modern societies sometimes fuelled by drug or alcohol abuse. Indeed, the Young Foundation report categorises vulnerable groups most likely to face severe needs as being migrants, runaways, sex workers, drug users, isolated older people, prisoners, dementia sufferers, school exclusions, looked after children, travellers and adults with neuro-development disorders.[44] But they face bigger challenges of their own with respect to social mobility and even purpose while existing within a legal and economic framework geared toward wealth creation and the protection of riches.

A Tarnished Legacy

The legacy of the baby boomers - years of consumption, work, political leadership and now retirement – has been profound. This most fortunate of generations enjoyed the benefits of the golden age of capitalism and was cushioned from the worst of periodic downturns including the most recent. While the global economic crisis represented a permanent loss of output and a significant strain on public finances, the magnitude of the political and economic response demonstrated how rich our societies have become. It showed the bubble in which we live today which separates us from both the poorest of the world, as well as our recent past. Being rich has its compensations of course and there is scant political desire to erode our wealth. But the nature of riches, the politics which support it and the societies it has created appears to have left an air of dissatisfaction. Riches are not simply material possessions. It is about a quality of life which naturally must be paid for. But one might expect that with the riches we have created over centuries and consolidated over decades, the developed world should now exist in some sort of advanced paradise. Our riches, which should strengthen our choice and wellbeing, in veracity, serve to reduce democratic freedom and even the power to enjoy our lives.

How did we get to this point? How did our ambitions become so narrow? It started with a policy consensus which pretty much all mainstream politicians signed up to. We can call this the 'mixed economic settlement'.

Chapter Three

The Mixed Economic Settlement

Can it be true that the politics we all experience is rooted in near irreversible and essentially conflicting forms of liberalism? Surveying the period since the end of the Second World War, it can be seen that contemporary politics has accepted an uneasy settlement of welfare liberalism, social liberalism and classical laissez-faire liberalism. For many of us, it is a mix, uneasy or not, that we embrace philosophically even though its seemingly permanent feature of policy offends our sense of democratic probity. And yet, modern liberal thought is neither engrained in our electorate[1] or indeed in the political parties which predominantly form governments in Europe or the United States.

Liberalism as it has broadly come to be regarded, in the tradition of John Stuart Mill – toleration, anti-authoritarianism, liberties, limitations on power, 'the harm principle'[2] - simply does not sit at the heart of what drives many prominent, democratic, political parties. In the United States, a country built on the liberalism of Thomas Paine, Republican and Democratic parties vie for middle-American, conservative, instincts. There have been exceptions and one might nod to the presidencies of Jackson and Roosevelt. But these are infrequent episodes in a long march of conservatism. A similar story can be told in Britain where the Liberal Democrat party (and its Liberal party ancestor) poll a consistent, respectable though usually always third position vote in successive elections over decades. And they have polled third to Conservative and Labour parties which could rarely be described as liberal. Again, there are exceptions. As Labour Home Secretary in the late 1960s, Roy Jenkins became one of the great liberal reformers; a feat which no subsequent Home Secretary has sought to emulate. The story is the same in continental Europe where student protests coincided with groundbreaking liberal reforms in Germany, France and elsewhere. And yet, the political settlement across these developed countries is one where such liberal facets are seemingly immovable objects. This means that leading politicians can be seen as pragmatic implementers of simply 'the way we do things round here'[3] rather than principled proponents. They pick from and pick at an economic and social settlement that few have the will, the initiative or the ability to change.

The United Kingdom straddles the two great powers of the United States and of Europe in more ways than the diplomatic tug of war between the so called 'special relationship' and the reality of geography, interests and membership. In the mixed economic settlement she sits as a direct compromise of both and so this part of the story will centre on the experience of Britain since the Second World War, drawing comparisons with the continent and America. In the twentieth century, European countries and the great United States accepted the idea that a mixed economy works best. There is barely a functional economy in the developed world which does not rely to some degree or other on a mix of private and public sectors. And although the term 'mixed economy' is perhaps most closely associated with ideas of the post-war consensus and a greater role for the state, the alternative of a truly free market economy with minimal government remains unrealistic; just as the ideal of a planned economy was shown to have failed with the downfall of Eastern communism. After all, Washington is home to one of the biggest governments in the world and certainly the most powerful. But, as the USA grew in international strength after the end of war, its traditional suspicion of big government led it to an economic mix which favoured greater self-reliance and was at the forefront of laissez-faire in the 1980s.

The vanquished (and the defeated) European powers of 1945 had little choice but to accept aid in the form of the Marshall Plan to reconstruct and to start again. Thus, Europeans built welfare systems funded by progressive taxation and clung on to their 'social democratic' attitudes over six decades. And Britain, a victor of war but destroyed economically and as a world power in 1945, started on the long road which was ever more to be attracted to the conflicting ideals of both mixed positions. Britain built a great welfare state in the latter 1940s, but elected and re-elected the most radical free market government in 1979 and the 1980s. As a result, when one compares taxation as a percentage of GDP between the USA and prominent EU countries or public spending, the United Kingdom sits snugly in the middle. In the pre-credit crunch year of 2006, taxation represented something like 44% of France's economy, 28% of America's and 37% of Britain's[4] with corresponding public spending priorities. Britain can therefore be said to represent the pinnacle (or the ultimate compromise) of the mixed economic settlement common to

Europe and the US. We have accepted a consensus on each of these contradictory liberal policies which the pendulum swing of government change is unable to alter in any substantial way. A reality all the more astounding given the weak hold that political liberalism has over those parties which regularly hold office. Indeed, the golden age of capitalism and its aftermath has formed a capitalist system into which we all buy; even though many people find it difficult to describe themselves so. And it is within this capitalist system that the mixed economic settlement, which includes welfarism, has been forged.

Welfare Legacy

When the 77 year old Winston Churchill returned to Downing Street in 1951, he was to head a substantially more far-reaching government than he had left six years before (notwithstanding the necessities of state power during conflict); one which consolidated in peace the domestic control government had required in war time. Despite national bankruptcy and ministerial exhaustion, Clement Attlee's administration, elected in a Labour landslide in 1945, had radically altered the idea of what the state did. Having endured the second long European war of the century, experienced its destruction on the nation and on the lives of its people, Britons in 1945 did not reject Churchill, the great war leader and statesman, because (as he saw it) they had 'such short memories', but rather because they had long ones stretching back to previous conflict and peace time strife. They remembered David Lloyd George's ambition and promise of reform after the Great War that never came amid (not dissimilar) economic crisis[5] and they remembered the experience of degradation during the depression of the 1930s which could have been avoided. They were also aware that Churchill's Conservatives would simply not have delivered this change and that a large part of the conservative establishment was implacably opposed to reform. 'Never Again' was Labour's simple yet powerful 1945 election slogan. Those two words were taken as the title for Peter Hennessy's history of the period.

> *Never again would there be war, never again would the British people be housed in slums, living off a meagre diet thanks to low wages or no wages at all; never again would mass unemployment blight the lives of millions; never again would natural abilities remain dormant in the absence of educational stimulus.*[6]

And so, in a frantic term of office, it was the first ever majority Labour government which delivered a National Health Service free at the point of delivery with 2688 hospitals placed under government control in 1948; an ambitious building programme creating more than 400,000 'homes fit for heroes' between 1946-48; the National Insurance Act of 1946 answered the clamour for old age pensions, unemployment sickness and funeral benefit, paid for by a levy on those in work; and a substantial nationalisation programme taking the Bank of England, railways, coal, road haulage, canals, utilities, iron and steel and Cable and Wireless into state control.

Central to the programme was a new settlement about what it is that the state does. And viewed from the twenty-first century, its long-term significance is profound. For the first time, healthcare was universal, the unemployed, the sick and the old received benefits, comprehensive education was available and compulsory[7] and universal child benefit supported and indeed fuelled that baby boom of the late 1940s. The state assumed a new role in ordinary people's lives 'from the cradle to the grave'. Anyone growing up in this New Jerusalem knew not a world where the state did not provide; they knew not the want of the 1930s. And while rationing continued until as late as 1954, while children with few toys played amongst the bomb sites and destruction of war, this new generation enjoyed comfortable housing, food on the table, doctors, dentists and opticians and a proper education. All this was provided for by the state.

Attlee's government delivered on a welfare blueprint set out in 1942 by the liberal economist, Sir William Beveridge, whose *Inter-departmental Committee on Social Insurance and Allied Services*, established under the war-time coalition, determined to tackle what was described as 'the five giants of want, disease, ignorance, squalor and idleness'. The Beveridge Report remains the most influential government white paper in contemporary British history. This was not to be a dusty, unread, unremarked upon government paper; second to the war itself, the Beveridge report was perhaps the most talked about contribution to public policy of its day. And if its liberalism were to be doubted, one only has to look to the Labour party whose initiative in government had instigated the Committee. With proposals quickly adopted by leaders of the Conservative and Liberal parties (though perhaps not the zeal of implementation that was to be associated with the Attlee government when it came two and a half years later), Labour leaders were reluctant. They were uneasy about national insurance and local and regional health administration, their instincts perhaps directed toward 'socialist' state planning.[8]

There was nothing plain sailing about the administration's programme implementation. Indeed, by 1947 things looked decidedly desperate. The harshest of winters, a fuel crisis, power cuts and weak industrial production followed by a severe Sterling crisis very nearly put a stop to these ambitious plans. And while the government eventually recovered its grip, its reputation had been tarnished. Nevertheless, the subsequent two and a half years were enough to not only complete the programme but to also create the first pillar of the mixed economic settlement by way of the post-war consensus.

The post-war Labour government represented a fantastic accomplishment, the benefits of which millions of Britons enjoy well into the twenty-first century. Attlee's legacy in contemporary history was cemented though, not only by the great achievements of his government but also because of the actions (or rather inaction) of the incoming Conservative government which was to remain in office until 1964. Despite its reticence in the creation of the welfare state, the Tories did nothing to undermine its existence. Governments led by Churchill, Anthony Eden, Harold Macmillan and (briefly) Alec Douglas Home accepted and supported the programme of 1945-51. In what became known as the post-war consensus, the period saw all major parties accept the welfare state, nationalised industries and Keynesian economics. And while consensus would be challenged by Edward Heath's Conservative government of 1970-74, come under severe pressure from the left during the Labour government of 1974-79 before being ideologically obliterated by Margaret Thatcher, the welfare legacy is just that. Welfare liberalism became a permanent fixture in political life. It became the first strand of the mixed economic settlement.

Beveridge and Keynes

Two of the great influences on the golden age of capitalism were liberal and radical. Beveridge and Keynes respectively were the intellectuals whose prowess dominated post-war capitalism. Beveridge was to draw the blueprint for the British welfare state, which when published as a government paper in 1942 found its way around the world. There was even a report about it discovered in Hitler's bunker as it was stormed by Russian troops in 1945 with an annotation that it represented a superior form of social insurance than anything dreamed in Germany.[9] John Maynard Keynes who died in 1946, on the other hand, was the architect of post war economic policy. An influential economist on both sides of the Atlantic before the war, his ideas were ingrained in Bretton Woods and the golden age of capitalism. And while Keynesianism became discredited amid the monetarist revolt, the general principles reappeared in response to our own credit crunch.

Both Victorians by birth and sometime academics and civil servants they nonetheless left a lasting imprint on the mixed economic settlement. Keynes a supporter of Lloyd George's 1929 campaign; Beveridge briefly a Liberal MP, both became identified with Labour in office. Intriguingly, their respective legacies survive to this day despite a battering by the free market ideology of the 1980s which brought its own contribution to the settlement. And here is what separates them from other, perhaps even more brilliant, contemporary scholars: for these two men, analysis and academic rigour was not enough. They wanted to change the world. And while their ideas respectively found fame after the Second World War, each had pursued their programmes, in one form or another, since the Great War. But in temperament these were very different men. Keynes was the more frolicsome and a consummate self-publicist. Married to a ballerina, he was nonetheless homosexual and a spirited member of the Bloomsbury set. William Beveridge was more conventional although his time was not confined to ivory towers. He worked with the Webbs as Sub-warden at Toynbee Hall in London's East End and was frequently involved in shaping legislation. They were both instrumental in forming lasting institutions which evolved into quite different looking beasts. Beveridge's were domestic welfare organisations centred around the National Health Service; Keynes helped design the great Washington institutions which exert such power to this day.

Obama's Healthcare Plot and Frau Merkel's Ambitions

Welfare is something more European in sentiment than American. It reflects different experiences of war and the golden age of capitalism: rebuilding free capitalism in continental Europe versus domineering world capitalism in the States. While Europe became more socially collective post war, the superpower of the United States, drenched like never before in the American dream, was confirmed in its belief in the individual. It has made a difference to our respective societies with European countries (and Scandinavia in particular) producing more coherent and equal systems. But for all the visions of what technology could do in our age for say healthcare, the truth remains that longevity is so often fixed at birth, determined by the relative wealth of one's parents. But the story too is less simplistic than that. The USA is as much a part of the mixed economic settlement as is Germany and France and recent experiences demonstrates this. Straddling the economic crisis which began in 2008, the experience of France and Germany on the one side of the Atlantic and the United States, refreshed (for a time at least) with the election of Barak Obama as President on the other, appears to offer some food for thought.

As global competition continued to put pressure on the fat and comfortable welfare states of Europe and following a period of relative economic under-performance in Germany (absorbing reunification) and France prior to credit crunch, there was a political trend in these nations toward cutting back on welfare spending. The reforms of Margaret Thatcher were becoming unlikely inspiration for politicians in 'old Europe' determined to make their economies attractive to overseas investors and reduce the stubbornly high unemployment numbers. Ahead of election back in 2005, the future German Chancellor, Angela Merkel, promised pretty radical reforms to weaken labour laws and shift the burden of unemployment insurance thereby lowering employment costs and making the economy more competitive. And it was that competition which sat at the centre of the programme since thousands of German jobs (traditionally in manufacturing and engineering) had seeped out to lower cost economies in South America, China and Eastern Europe in particular. But while Western European countries ostensibly attempted to move closer to the US – or more precisely the UK which at the time seemed to be the model – there was impetus in the US to complete President Clinton's failed healthcare reforms. Barak Obama's electoral promise and administrative success was to extend health cover to the estimated fifty million Americans heretofore without support. While the debate in the States became caricatured by the extremes and personified by Sarah Palin's talk of 'Obama Death Panels', the truth was far more sophisticated and essentially not about an aversion to welfare. Typically, it was *The Economist* which summed up the moral issues which sat at the heart of this policy. 'Health reformers always smash up against two unpalatable truths. We are all going to die. And the demand for interventions that might postpone that day far outstrips supply. No politician would be caught dead admitting this, of course: most promise that all will receive whatever is medically necessary. But what does that mean? Should doctors seek to save the largest number of lives, or the largest years of life? Even in America, resources are finite.'[10]

In rebuilding society after the war, Attlee was not faced with such dilemmas or at least not on this scale. Healthcare has advanced rapidly, health needs are infinite and the growth in our riches since those days mean that for some (indeed for many), medical services go far beyond the needs envisaged in 1942. Were Beveridge to publish a report today, he would be faced with the same dilemmas which the Obama administration had to grapple. Similarly, in Germany were the architects of the post war welfare system to revisit today's environment, they might seek to temper its effects. Here we see the continuity between systems and these simultaneous reforms showing welfare policy drawing closer together. It demonstrates how welfare forms part of the mixed economic settlement.

The Market Knows Best

It was in Britain too that consensus politics were to be challenged as the golden age of capitalism gave way to economic decline as the 1960s slipped into the 1970s. First the technocratic Conservative Prime Minister Edward Heath tried but retreated and then, after further strains under the Wilson/Callaghan government, a woman came to power in Britain who wanted to 'change everything'.

Monetarism had first seen the light of day in Britain in 1976 when, forced to take a conditional loan from the International Monetary Fund, Labour Chancellor Denis Healey adhered to the strict rules imposed upon his Treasury. The public sector borrowing requirement was slashed and the government accepted formal targets for the supply of money and the expansion of domestic credit. While the British economy accrued the benefits of this new discipline, Healey accrued no equivalent political dividend. As Edmund Dell points out, the 'resentments were piling up against the man who had sold socialism to the IMF'.[11] The left within Labour not only rejected Healey's monetary obedience but were ready to reject the pragmatic Keynesianism of the consensus.

Margaret Thatcher was to have different ideas. The one-time Education Secretary had snatched the Conservative party leadership from the disgruntled Heath in a 1975 coup which became known as 'the peasants' revolt'. Thatcher had come to represent the new right faction of the Conservative party to which she and fellow former minister Keith Joseph (known as the 'Mad Monk' even to his friends) had become conscripted after defeat at the polls in 1974. 'It was only in April 1974 that I was converted to Conservatism',[12] Joseph wrote. But of course this was not conservatism. It did not believe in conserving or preserving. These were radical, liberal, ideologues who demanded radical, dogmatic change.

Joseph sat in Edward Heath's Cabinet along with Margaret Thatcher and watched as the government's economic policy fell apart. They saw the consensus challenged, policy u-turn, the lack of resolve, the lack of ideological commitment. They also saw their party thrown out of office.

In that very same year of 1974 Thatcher and Joseph helped establish the Centre for Policy Studies, a think tank that would champion what was to be their new economic thinking. It was a bold move for two people still bound by collective decision making. As a member of Heath's Shadow Cabinet in opposition, Joseph was openly critical of their collective record in office and it was during these strained months he gave his now famous Stockton lecture on the economy entitled *Monetarism IS Not Enough* (eventually published in 1976). Here he contrasted what he described as the wealth producing sectors of the economy (the private sector) with wealth consuming sectors (government and the public sector). He argued that the economy suffers as its wealth producing sectors shrink and expounded his belief that the state had tried to do too much and what it did, it did so badly.

These proponents of 'new conservatism' repudiated Keynes's demand management and the incomes policies which had dogged the Callaghan government. They took hold of the argument that it was expansion of the money supply that was responsible for inflation and it was this that should be at the heart of policy. They had adopted monetarism, they had adopted it absolutely and they dragged it into office having won, quite decisively, the 1979 general election.

It was this conviction politics which set the Thatcher years apart from her predecessors or successors in office. Famous for her 'U-turn if you want to, the lady's not for turning' speech in 1980, Thatcher did not buckle as Heath had done in the face of rising unemployment and stuck doggedly to even failing policies as joblessness hit a staggering three million. In a ruthless break from consensus politics, which had emphasised the need to create full employment, tackling inflation and allowing market freedom was now the prime economic objective of the government. The tool for doing this was not to be fiscal policy, taxation and public spending which had characterised the actions of the Treasury for the previous thirty years, but rather it was monetary policy, the control of the money supply and interest rates.[13]

While it might have come as a shock to many in Britain, the 1979 manifesto had set out the argument that, 'to master inflation, proper monetary discipline is essential, with publicly stated targets for the rate of growth of the money supply. At the same time, a gradual reduction in the size of the Government's borrowing requirement is also vital.'[14] And good as its word, the government set out to achieve just that by establishing strict targets to reduce money supply as part of that was called the Medium Term Financial Strategy (MTFS), which was unveiled in March 1980. Unfortunately, and contrary to popular opinion, it did not work.

The new Chancellor of the Exchequer, Geoffrey Howe, tightened monetary and fiscal control and floated the exchange rate in his first Budget in 1979. Paradoxically, that abolition of exchange controls meant that 'the country lost the ability to pursue an independent monetary policy, and quantitative monetary aggregates became even less reliable as an indicator of the government's macroeconomic policy than before.'[15] And facing both deficit and increasing public spending, the government cut income tax and practically doubled VAT to

15%. As one critical insider, Ian Gilmour, put it: 'All in all the first budget of the anti-inflation crusaders propelled the retail price index upwards by almost six percentage points... Yet the government's overriding economic aim was to lower inflation, and most people are fairly aware that the best way to bring inflation down is not to put prices up.'[16] The problem was that as part of the MTFS, the Treasury selected the relatively wide measure of money supply, M3, as its target which includes lending, credit and, vitally, savings. M3 proved to be sensitive to interest rates though largely hopeless in the battle against inflation. And so as interest rates rose in an effort to tighten monetary policy, savings naturally grew, ironically leading to an expansion in the money supply, M3.

Business, which was suffering from the ill effects of oil price rises, began to borrow. But because of inflation they were cautious and tended to borrow only short-term. Britain's short-term yet high interest rate attracted speculative flows from overseas. 'International speculators not only diversified into a widely traded petro-currency; they could get 17 per cent interest as well.'[17] The result was continued expansion in M3 which rapidly grew out of control.[18] Inflation and unemployment went up. Contrary to the new Thatcherite economic theory, the situation did not lead to a fall in wages beyond that resulting from job losses. Instead there was a rise in social security payments, which in turn undermined cuts in public expenditure.[19] Deindustrialisation, especially in the North, set in. Growth was sluggish or non-existent. Research and development declined.[20] Relative to previous decades or by comparison to Europe and the USA, Britain's economic performance was indisputably poor.[21]

Why tell this story about policy failure? The facts are that it did not work but that it did not matter that it did not work. Much like the travails of the Attlee government, despite such shortcomings in detail, the government succeeded in changing the rules of the game; rules which were perhaps not entirely perfected until the lady herself had left office. Policy shifted from the state to the market, from demand to supply side economics.   Exchange controls were abolished and Britain opened up its economy to the world. After re-election in 1983, a programme of privatisation returned one nationalised industry after another to the private sector.   And while this policy area did not have the dogmatic zeal that retrospect would afford (the first sale of 51% of British Telecom was a pragmatic attempt to inject funds into the telecoms industry without breaking public sector borrowing rules), it changed fundamentally the idea of what the private and public sectors should do.

By the time Margaret Thatcher left office, some forty state owned businesses had been sold. The programme shrank the publicly owned proportion of Gross Domestic Product from 12% in 1979 to 2% by the turn of the century. Along the way, her government deregulated the City of London's financial markets in what became known as 'big bang' in 1986; a new market led industry was re-born.   The failure of the 1970s meant that Thatcher's children would accept the market as king.   It was the market which knew best, which allocated resources most efficiently and which supported economic growth.   And quite fundamentally for the health of our riches today, the 1980s meant that the state's role in promoting equality was not only diminished but there was a view held amongst the true believers that (almost echoing Gordon

Gekko's 'greed is good'), inequality was perhaps now a positive force which stimulated enterprise and economic growth. The period even gained an 'ism' all of its own: 'Thatcherism'.

And these reforms which the Thatcher government hammered through, became of fundamental importance to the mixed economic settlement, not only because of their radical nature, but also because more than twenty years after the eponymous leader of this economic revolt left office, her successors have done nothing to undermine her legacy. Indeed if Thatcher's greatest achievement was Tony Blair, a man who not only accepted the market and privatisation but who was prepared to extend them, then the philosophy had moved from dogma to pragmatic mainstream.

But what of the arguments about the great Attlee consensus? What of this powerful case that the achievements of that reforming Labour government have become fundamental to the mixed economy settlement of Britain? Thatcher, it is true, undid the policies of economic management and state ownership of industry that formed part of the long-lived achievements of that government. But it was welfare that was at the very heart of that programme and though she might have wanted to dismantle Britain's welfare state, even a government as radical as hers and with such large majorities did not destroy, fundamentally at least, this tenet of Attlee's legacy. And for all her forcefulness, an early attempt to undermine the National Health Service was swiftly dismissed as Ian Gilmour, Cabinet 'wet' and reliable chronicler of the era testifies:

In September 1982 the Central Policy Review Staff circulated a paper to Cabinet on the prime minister's authority. Amongst radical schemes to end the public funding of higher education and slash social security budget was the momentous proposal to replace the NHS with personally paid for private health insurance and to charge patients for visiting a doctor. Among the nation's institutions, only the monarchy was more popular than the National Health Service. So when the CPRS was leaked to The Economist under the heading 'Thatcher's Holocaust' [18 September 1982], Mrs Thatcher was forced reluctantly to retreat and to disassociate herself from such dangerous suggestions. The electorate was assured that the NHS was safe in the government's hands.[22]

Thatcher then, added a vital piece of liberalism to the mixed economic settlement and in tearing down some of the tenants of the post war consensus, in turn cemented in place the welfare legacy bequeathed by Attlee. She might have instinctively detested the welfare state, and personally (and proudly) chose private health care, but in the sweep of history her policies, radical as they were, represented a new policy consensus running parallel to the older.

Reagan and Thatcher

The year after Margaret Thatcher assumed office in Britain, Ronald Reagan won the 1980 US presidential election. These two world leaders, with their very different backgrounds nonetheless were to become political soul mates during the 1980s and their personal relationship and shared prejudices came to dominate the policy agenda. They had met in 1975, while he was Governor of California and shortly after she had grabbed the Conservative party leadership from Edward Heath. This was four years before she would assume the premiership and a year before he would narrowly lose the Republican presidential nomination to incumbent Gerald Ford. We know now how symbiotic they became during this tumultuous decade but it is clear that there was a spark from the first. Believed to be their first correspondence, Reagan's handwritten note, 'Dear Mrs Thatcher', dated April 30 1975, thanked her for being 'so generous with your time... you were very kind and I am grateful… Mrs Reagan and I would like very much to return your hospitality. In the meantime please know you have an enthusiastic supporter out here in the 'colonies.''[23] At the other end of their relationship, Thatcher's 2004 eulogy to the former President was heartfelt: 'We have lost a great president, a great American, and a great man. And I have lost a dear friend. In his lifetime Ronald Reagan was such a cheerful and invigorating presence that it was easy to forget what daunting historic tasks he set himself.'[24]

They were an unlikely pairing. Both had worked their way up from modest backgrounds and ironically each had 'lived above the shop' in their childhoods, with Reagan's family taking an apartment above the HC Pitney Variety store in Tampico while Thatcher's lived above her father's grocery store in Grantham. When they moved into accommodation above the White House and Downing Street respectively, each would quip about again 'living above the shop'. But the similarities end there. He was glamorous, loved sports and was attracted to Hollywood; she was austere, details driven and frankly terrifying. Reagan's self-deprication knew no ends, just as Thatcher's knew no beginning. He would joke 'I have left orders to be awakened at any time in case of national emergency - even if I'm in a Cabinet meeting' and, 'It's true hard work never killed anybody, but I figure, why take the chance?' Thatcher on the other hand was a rather humourless workaholic who survived on a reputed four hours sleep a night. Nevertheless, she once described Reagan as 'the second most important man in my life'.[25] Opposites really do attract.

Like Thatcher, he had a dogmatic zeal for rolling back the frontiers of the state but over the eight years of his Presidency only managed to reduce federal spending from 22 per cent to 21 percent of GDP.[26] In Britain, spending slowed but, as Gilmour points out, in real terms 'never rose by less than 1 percent a year between 1979 and 1990, and at election times it rose by over 4 percent. Thus despite cumulative underfunding, the structure of the welfare state remained largely intact.'[27] But it was by a very large margin, force of personality and ideological conviction which defined these two politicians' contribution to the politics of those years and the mixed economic settlement.

The Blairite 'Compromise'

It is said that Margaret Thatcher's greatest achievement was Tony Blair. By the time the young Tony became Labour leader upon the untimely death of John Smith in 1994, his party had travelled a huge distance. Only eleven years before, under the hapless Michael Foot, Labour had contested the 1983 election on manifesto commitments ('the longest suicide note in history' according to Gerald Kaufman) to nationalise industry, punitively tax the rich, withdraw from Europe and unilateral nuclear disarmament. But Blair was able to confidently scrap

Clause IV of Labour's constitution which committed the party to the socialist aim of the common ownership of the means of production, re-brand as *New* Labour and embrace the economic reforms of Thatcherism. The compromise, such as it was, centred on accepting and indeed extending the New Public Management model of public service provision begun in the 1980s but crucially the government simultaneously increased spending on the sector. Under Thatcher, business techniques were drawn into the management of public services.

Roy Griffiths of the supermarket chain Sainsbury's kicked it off when he was asked to examine the NHS. Intriguingly, he made the crucial point that in private sector organisations, at least when one considers those below board level, the simplistic goal of profit making is not a great motivator and makes little difference to how people they do their job. But he famously commented that 'if Florence Nightingale were carrying her lamp through the corridors of the NHS today she would almost certainly be searching for the people in charge'.

The Griffiths Report led to a new form of general management in the NHS and subsequently throughout other public service bodies. It meant a change away from comfortable, 'administration' towards 'management' style of business. This meant traditional managerial hierarchy and a division of labour which had a lasting impact in terms of outward orientation and internal efficiency. 'New Labour had an ambivalent attitude, however, to "new public management". They continued the "managerialist" institutions which they inherited from the Conservatives... Yet they supplanted the last surviving pretensions of the "new public management" towards diminished political interference and devolution of responsibility to and down the management chain.'[28] New

Public Management, then, represents the collaboration of these conflicting forms of liberalism but also the clash of these distinctive ideological aims. It embraced the idea of the citizen as consumer rather than subservient to a centralised state and it enthusiastically employed the qualities of the market in the delivery of welfare. But it did so with public funding and ever greater centralised management which did not absolve the state of responsibility or allow the market itself to seize control. New Public Management as it developed under the Blair administration is a glue which held together these competing ideological visions but did little to contribute to or indeed extend ideological thinking.

The Liberati on my Back

The oldest of the baby boomers were twenty three years old when half a million strong gathered at the White Lake dairy farm to enjoy thirty-two acts, including Jimi Hendrix, The Grateful Dead and Janis Joplin, at what was to become the infamous Woodstock Festival. The festival, 'three days of peace and music' taking place in August 1969, came at the end of a culturally charged decade which rebelled against conservatism and social repression. In many ways it reflects the attitudes of these baby boomers who had enjoyed the relative prosperity of the post-war world. As they became independent, the stuffy and repressed 1950s turned momentously into the libertine swinging sixties. The contraceptive pill which appeared in 1960 revolutionised sexual attitudes; recreational drugs became far more widespread; fashions all the more outrageous; popular music which older generations found offensive became the staple sound to this very day.

Bob Dylan, who had declined an invitation to play at Woodstock, perhaps personifies the merging of music and liberal counter-culture during the sixties. His protest songs against war in Vietnam, nuclear weapons, and against racism in the south of his own United States had an intellectual importance which left most of his chart topping contemporaries wanting. Dylan was part of the 1963 March on Washington where Martin Luther King delivered his most famous speech, telling the assembled crowds that, 'I have a dream that my four little children will one day live in a nation where they will not be judged by the color of their skin, but by the content of their character.'

This was a generation which, driven by popular culture, fashion, drugs and technology, was destined for a social clash with what it saw as the 'conservative establishment'. In contrast to the peace and love of Woodstock, this clash became angry, and notably May 1968 saw student riots and strikes in Paris. This represented a revolt against the very consumer society which the baby boomers had had enjoyed for a decade and would continue to exploit into their retirement.

But it was that establishment which delivered on some of the most far-reaching liberal, social change in Europe and the United States alike. And while they accepted it as part of the settlement, politicians for years to come would criticise what those changes meant: including the baby boomers themselves when they won office.

In July 2004, Tony Blair prematurely heralded the 'end of the 1960s liberal, social consensus on law and order.' Launching his government's five year strategy on the criminal justice system, Blair took the opportunity to deride the achievements of liberalism in the 1960s, blaming the ills of modern Britain on this progressive decade, rather than the increasingly authoritarian developments since. [29]

> *It was John Stuart Mill who articulated the modern concept that with freedom comes responsibility. But in the 1960's revolution, that didn't always happen. Law and order policy still focused on the offender's rights, protecting the innocent, understanding the social causes of their criminality. All through the 1970s and 1980s, under Labour and Conservative Governments, a key theme of legislation was around the prevention of miscarriages of justice. Meanwhile some took the freedom without the responsibility. The worst criminals became better organised and more violent. The petty criminals were no longer the bungling but wrong-headed villains of old; but drug pushers and drug-abusers, desperate and without any residual moral sense. And a society of different lifestyles spawned a group of young people who were brought up without parental discipline, without proper role models and without any sense of responsibility to or for others. All of this was then multiplied in effect, by the economic and social changes that altered the established pattern of community life in cities, towns and villages throughout Britain and throughout the developed world. Here, now, today, people have had enough of this part of the 1960s consensus.*[30]

Blair's was a complex and contradictory liberal attitude. He was the prime minister who introduced and celebrated civil partnerships and freedom of information[31] but who also fervently supported the introduction of identity cards and the DNA database. He was criticising the zenith of post war liberal government, epitomised by Roy Jenkins' tenure at the Home Office during the late 1960s. Criticised as promoting 'the permissive society', Jenkins brought about a series of the most momentous legislative changes and attitudes in domestic policy of the period. The achievements are staggering and include: Removal of prison flogging, decriminalisation of homosexuality (1967), an end to the Lord Chamberlain's power to censor London theatres ('I've always thought it has been very difficult to show that preventing people reading things improved their morals.'[32]), legalisation of abortion (1968), and liberalisation of divorce law (1969). If these were the main acts, there were further changes in temperament including a 'civilising' of immigration (eventually leading to a Race Relations Act under successor James Callaghan), prison population reduction and parole independence, improved legal aid, firearms licences and the introduction of majority jury verdicts. 'I see the central purpose of the Home Office as being that of striking a very difficult balance between the need to preserve the Queen's peace and the need to preserve the liberty of the individual... I see the central purpose of the Home Office as holding this balance between liberty and order.' Jenkins put it in 1966.[33]

This was a decade which was to see momentous civil liberty developments in the United States too. After Kennedy's assassination and Johnson's elevation to the Presidency, three of the most important contemporary legislative Acts were passed: Civil Rights Act (1964), the National Voting Rights Act (1965), and the Civil rights Act (1968). These laws outlawed racial segregation and state discrimination, still prevalent in the south, ended discrimination in voting qualification, and outlawed racial discrimination in housing. In addition, the legislative programme included the Economic Opportunity Act (1964) which created the jobs corp, the community action program and the college work study programme all aimed at creating greater social mobility; there was the Elementary and Secondary Education Act (1965) and the Higher Education Act (1965); the Voting Rights Act (1965); the Model Cities Act (1966); the Fair Housing Act (1968), to name just a selection. In 1964 Johnson 'declared war on poverty' to substantial popular support and set in train a short period of liberal reform which encompassed this legislative agenda and whose impact was one of the most significant and long lasting of contemporary social history. The historian of the period Kent Germany put is so:

With the War on Poverty, American liberalism's insistent optimism and deep faith in expertise met head-on a domestic crisis of race, social order, and political economy comparable in scope only to the Civil War and the Great Depression. The administrations of President John Kennedy and his successor Lyndon Johnson became the primary organizers of the governmental response to that crisis. To deal with concern that poverty threatened American progress, their administrations pushed hard for economic growth that could create full employment and for social reform

> *that could enable the poor to access what President*
> *Johnson called "the good life."*[34]

And so, despite subsequent rhetoric by the baby boomers in office, there was a third strain of liberal policy which has come to be unchallenged. As that baby boom generation protested and rebelled, the 1960s pursued a socially liberalising agenda like no other in our lifetimes. It civilised society but broke down the barriers to wealth and status. Nevertheless it became part of the mixed economic settlement.

Roy Jenkins

One of Roy Jenkins best day's work was when in 1965 he had a refrigerated drinks cabinet dragged into his Home Office. Jenkins had a well known taste for claret which he would drink by the English pint over lunch. But this was no frivolous move by the young Home Secretary[35] because it replaced an indicator board on which the names of condemned prisoners were moved gradually towards their date of execution.

A few years before, Jenkins had authored a book[36] about reforming the Home Office centred around abolition of the death penalty which was still common in 1950s Britain just as it is in the United States today. Capital punishment was abolished just before Jenkins arrived in his new office, the result of a private members bill and a free vote in the Commons. But it was Roy who was seen as the motivating force behind it. In an interview with Robin Day in 1966, he admitted, 'I would have found it an almost intolerable burden to be Home Secretary had one had to decide whether or not people were to be hanged.'[37]

Jenkins was unusual in that he was a progressive Home Secretary, the likes of which the country had rarely seen before or since. In a polity in which the progressive nature of Home Secretaries is confined to the trend whereby they become progressively more authoritarian, Jenkins was the anomaly. To a significant degree of course, he was reflecting the mood of his times but perhaps only he would have had the vision and determination to have made such a momentous, courageous and liberal change to British society so soon and so decisively. In nearly half a century of retrospect many would ask why it did not continue.

Jenkins was one of the most principled, big beast, figures of post-war British politics. He put it to Day that 'I think there's nothing more humiliating than someone who advocates views when they have complete freedom and no responsibility and becomes an utterly different person when they have responsibility.'[38] A polymath, he successfully held the Chancellorship after devaluation in the late 1960s, became President of the European Commission in the 1970s, formed his own Social Democratic Party in the 1980s, was awarded the Order of Merit, became Chancellor of Oxford, leader of his Liberal Democrat party in the Lords, enjoyed food, wine, socialising, literature and was an outstanding author of biography comprising figures from Churchill to Roosevelt.

He was one of a band of leading politicians of the period who had seen war at first hand and that experience had shaped his views; especially with regards to the case for a united Europe. A future prime minister who never was, his stand when deputy leader of the Labour party to vote against his party whip in favour of Britain's entry to the European Economic Community served his country well but not his own career.   To vote as he did meant resigning the deputy leadership and when Harold Wilson eventually quit as leader (and prime Minister) in 1976 having returned his party to government, Roy came a disappointing third in the contest to replace him. But it was precisely the principle which prevented him from becoming PM which meant that he had such an impact on the political theatre in which he operated.

He spanned the mixed economic settlement having started his parliamentary career in 1948 just as the NHS began its life. Interestingly Jenkins' father, Arthur, was principal private secretary to Attlee himself and briefly a minister in his government.   Roy sat at the centre of politics throughout the post-war consensus as Labour politician, delivering the socially liberal reforms of the 1960s. A Keynesian by instinct, his SDP nonetheless made the free market transition between consensus and Thatcherism.   And in later life he was mentor to Tony Blair and his early aim of 'big tent' politics.

The Mixed Economic Settlement

Our post-war world developed and entrenched three fundamental and contrasting forms of liberalism into our politics and into our societies.   The great welfare state, epitomised by the Attlee administration remains to this day; politicians across the world accept pragmatically the supremacy of the market as readily as Margaret Thatcher promoted it philosophically; and our societies and our laws are more socially liberal, more tolerant and less discriminatory for the reforms of the 1960s. Perhaps in part is was the way these reforms were implemented that gave them longevity. Attlee chose a liberal rather than socialist approach to the welfare state. And Thatcher ensured that none of her successors would dismantle the principle of public healthcare with her forced retreat into the adage that the 'NHS is safe in my hands'; a slogan which would be repeated by her less idealistically committed heirs.

Ironically, she paved the way for this type of 'contamination politics' in the early 1970s when, as Education Secretary, she ended free school milk for seven to eleven year olds. Such was the unpopularity of the move accompanied by the indelible slogan of 'Thatcher, Thatcher, Milk Snatcher', that irrespective of the health or economic case, no subsequent government has been able or willing to remove provision from the remainder of schoolchildren. Indeed, health minister Ann Milton's suggestion that it was an 'ineffective universal measure' in August 2010 caused a media and political furore and had to be stamped on by Downing Street which insisted there would be no change in policy. Such is politics that policy can become ingrained.

Beyond the incrementalism discussed later in this book, however, the social liberal reforms of the 1960s enjoyed no such similar pivot which is perhaps why civil liberties suffer the most consistent attacks of any part of the mixed economic settlement. Nevertheless, each of these strands forms part of the mixed economic settlement which dominates our lives into the twenty first century. The futurologists of the 1950s did not foresee this mix which has been as successful as any in the history of the world at providing for its people. To some degree it is ideologically inconsistent. But each strand has shaped our second decade destiny and is self-supporting. Some advances are only possible because of or in their own way have created economic growth. But the mixed economic settlement remains an incomplete project. While the years to follow saw politics coalesce around the settlement, the project failed to offer a political strand. With two decades of acceptance, our priorities became about accumulating wealth not what we can do with a rich society for ourselves or the outside world. This book offers a step in the direction of completing the project by way of a political defrayal, but just how and who is to blame for accepting this settlement on our behalf is the subject of the next chapter.

Chapter Four

Decades of Acceptance

The final decade of the twentieth century and the opening decade of the twenty-first century were notable for many things. They represent both continuity and contrast; harmony and conflict. The 1990s were years of relative stability for the West which basked in the ideological victory of the cold war. The collective anxiety of nuclear Armageddon dissolved into care-free individual anxieties of global unimportance. Meanwhile the pace of globalisation and interdependence quickened, drenching the world in a commonality of experience. And for the generation of politicians who presided over these years, that victory was all the more significant. For the stewards of these two decades had the social consequences of one great bloody ideological conflict and the collective pressures of the brinkmanship of another impressed deep into their psyches.

The end of the Second World War had created the world with which they identified, the cold war had made it a matter of ideology and the collapse of the Berlin Wall had told them they were right. It is this experience which made the mixed economic settlement not only possible but a policy concoction without rival. These two decades have been the ones which too have bred the worst obsession with our riches with all that has meant for weakened politics and society. These decades witnessed the decline in common purpose, a suspension in ideology and a blind acceptance of the mixed economic settlement amid benign economic conditions.

To blame is the baby boomer generation of politicians who were characterised by a new easy style, an entrenched almost post-ideological attitude, and a confidence in their actions. The practicalities of a shrinking world in both communications and thought has also meant that politicians across the developed world have become more alike; the product of similar experiences, schooling at one of a relatively small number of interconnected universities, and a narrow choice of pre-politics careers centring around the law or indeed policy.

But today there is a new generation, a post-baby boom generation, of world leaders who are re-casting the settlement within the context of global interdependence. Their experiences are even closer than those of the baby boomers; they are even less likely to have serious careers behind them before running for office and they appear supremely comfortable in the political clothes they wear and share.

The Baby Boomers win Office

The biggest baby boomer of them all was Bill Clinton, a man who would come to embody his generation – for reasons ill as well as good. With his high political ideals and low personal morals Clinton shook the cage of dignified perceptions of the presidency. Not only were his numerous sexual encounters (and lies to cover them up) played out before the world, but this media savvy politician seemed to treat high office with less respect than his predecessors had, at least appeared to have, done.[1] Clinton ate burgers washed down with Diet Coke, wore a sweat shirt and baseball cap in the Oval Office, was watched by millions as he played the saxophone in dark glasses on the *Arsenio Hall Show*, 'experimented with marijuana a time or two… [but] didn't inhale',[2] and famously told a White House press briefing: 'I did not have sexual relations with that woman, Miss Lewinsky.' When, of course, he did. This was the baby boomer commander in chief. 'Indeed', as Joe Klein put it, 'Bill Clinton often seemed the apotheosis of his generation's alleged sins: the moral relativism, the tendency to pay more attention to marketing than to substance, the solipsistic callowness'.[3] At his presidential inauguration in January 1993, the voice of the 1960s counter-culture himself, Bob Dylan, performed *Chimes of Freedom* (Tolling for the rebel, tolling for the rake, Tolling for the luckless, the abandoned an' forsaked, Tolling for the outcast, burnin' constantly at stake…') on the steps of the Lincoln Memorial. It was a showy, brash affair; a celebration of the candidate who some called 'Elvis', others 'Bubba'. And in his address the new President told listeners:

Today, a generation raised in the shadows of the Cold War assumes new responsibilities in a world warmed by the sunshine of freedom but threatened by still ancient hatreds and new plagues….

Our democracy must not only be the envy of the world but the engine of our own renewal. There is nothing wrong with America that cannot be fixed by what is right with America….

...our greatest strength is the power of our ideas, which are still new in many lands. Across the world, we see them embraced – and we rejoice. Our hopes, our hearts, our hands, are with those on every continent who are building democracy and freedom. Their cause is America's cause.[4]

It was an address which, with twenty years of hindsight, appears as prophetic as it seems naive. After all, it reflected the complacent, and ultimately misplaced, belief that American ideals had not only emphatically 'won' to the exclusion of all others in the world. But it also foretold the fear of new threats from 'ancient hatreds', something which did not impress itself on the conscience of ordinary Americans until Clinton had left office eight years later. But here, in the United States in 1993, the transition to baby boomer was all the more noticeable, not because of a radical shift in policy but rather due to the change in attitude which served to narrow our economic destiny.

It was such a noticeable generational change since Clinton's rather dignified predecessor, George H.W. Bush, was a man of quite a different era; the implications of which Clinton had exploited during the election campaign (there was even a (false) story that Bush was unaware of supermarket scanners[5]). Whether or not he was out of touch is less important than the historical differences between the 41st and 42nd Presidents. After all, Bush had become a naval aviator in 1942, remaining in the military until war had ended in September 1945. It was just eleven months later that a bouncing Bill Clinton entered the world, one of the original baby boomers.

The first true baby boomer to win the highest office in the land in Britain was a youthful Tony Blair, taking office in 1997 at the age of 43. But perhaps his predecessor, John Major, born in 1943 and taking office in 1990 might claim the spiritual prize as the first prime minister to have grown up in the post-war world and to have enjoyed the benefits of the golden age of capitalism.

But Major appeared as far more old fashioned and unexciting, having more in common with President Bush than Clinton and this was reflected in their personal relations. Indeed, there is not a whiff of the new freedoms of the 1960s in his autobiography, where the young Major spent the decade of love and dissent speaking on a Brixton Market soapbox in somewhat 1860s style.[6] The young Tony Blair, on the other hand, modelled himself on Mick Jagger and early photographs show him with unkempt, long hair and the lippy sneer of the Stones' front man. An electric guitarist, at Oxford Blair eschewed politics in favour of his rock band, *The Ugly Rumours*, and was later a promoter. In parallels with Clinton's new type of President, which previous British prime minister (contrived as it was) had walked into Downing Street with a ministerial red box in one hand, a guitar case in the other?

Blair though was perhaps of higher personal morality than Clinton and, somewhat unusually in increasingly secular Europe, wore his Christian beliefs on his sleeve (The Ugly Rumours was a Christian band). 'We don't do God' was the rather dismissive warning of his one time Director of Communications, Alistair Campbell. But Blair refused to keep his faith hidden seeming to take the rather tautological view that 'I do the right things because I am a Christian; because I am a Christian, what I do is the right thing'. This baby boom premiere, who had only known a peaceful Europe, committed more British troops to war than any of his predecessors since

Winston Churchill himself; all in the name of the kind of politics in which he believed: protecting the rich society he has only ever known.

This marked him out from many of the influential political figures of 1970s and 1980s British politics including Edward Heath, Denis Healey and Roy Jenkins whose own experiences of conflict had united them in revulsion of war (and in an attraction to the peace of Europe). Theirs was a more comprehensive vision of peace, cooperation and a quality of life. Indeed, for Heath, the only one of these three who made it to Number 10, 'undoubtedly felt that his triumph in taking Britain into the Community represented not only a great success but a permanent one too, the end of a process that so many of his wartime generation, just like their European contemporaries, saw as the unfinished business of the Second World War – Jenkins, Healey and Crosland on one side, Heath, Barber and Whitelaw on the other.'[7] This was a generation of politicians which understood the horrors of armed conflict at first hand. They avoided war and refused to follow the Americans into the ill-fated Vietnam. Blair and his generation had no such misgivings.

Under-reported but politically explosive was the so called 'Blair doctrine' set out in a speech to the Chicago Economics Club as early as 1999. With Kosovo in the back of his mind and eighteen months before fellow boomer George W. Bush was sworn in as President and all that would come to mean for their combustible foreign policy partnership, Tony Blair told his American audience:

> *...we may be tempted to think back to the clarity and simplicity of the Cold War. But now we have to*

establish a new framework. No longer is our existence as states under threat. Now our actions are guided by a more subtle blend of mutual self interest and moral purpose in defending the values we cherish. In the end values and interests merge. If we can establish and spread the values of liberty, the rule of law, human rights and an open society then that is in our national interests too. The spread of our values makes us safer. As John Kennedy put it 'Freedom is indivisible and when one man is enslaved who is free?'

The most pressing foreign policy problem we face is to identify the circumstances in which we should get actively involved in other people's conflicts. Non-interference has long been considered an important principle of international order. And it is not one we would want to jettison too readily. One state should not feel it has the right to change the political system of another or foment subversion or seize pieces of territory to which it feels it should have some claim. But the principle of non-interference must be qualified in important respects. Acts of genocide can never be a purely internal matter. When oppression produces massive flows of refugees which unsettle neighbouring countries then they can properly be described as 'threats to international peace and security'.[8]

While the potential unpopularity of conflict was something from which Clinton, a Vietnam draft dodger, shied away, the implications of the Blair Doctrine, global intervention and regime change, were embraced by Bush after 2001. It represents an ingrained belief that the 'half' of the world which won the cold war, those who had enjoyed the benefits of the mixed economic settlement, were unequivocally right and those who contradicted its principles even where they presented no direct threat to the West were both wrong and legitimate military targets. The priority for this generation extended little further than protecting our riches and employing the considerable might of a developed country to do so.

The world really was black and white, good and evil, cowboys and indians, for baby boom President George W. Bush. And once the horrific 2001 attacks on New York had fulfilled Clinton's 'ancient hatreds and new plagues' prophecy, he spoke in terms of the world being split as such. 'You're either with us or you're with the terrorists' he warned friend and foe alike. For Europeans pompously bewildered at Bush's popularity at home, mocking his inelegant strangling of the English language might be sufficient explanation. Bush seemed not to think before he spoke, but such honest, unpolished 'straight talking' was a welcome contrast with his 'Slick Willy' predecessor who had consulted focus groups on everything from the heights of his policy programme to the trivialities of his holiday destinations. And in any case, however unrefined, it was a message nonetheless with which a baby boom electorate identified.

Ironically, that change of style from slick PR to a baby boom, 'dogmatic' assault was achieved in one fell swoop in Britain. A pupil of Clinton, Tony Blair was elected with minimal ideological baggage, a scion of the focus groups. In Iraq and the so-called 'war on terror' he not only discovered a policy in which he believed, irrespective of the millions of voters who marched in protest, but also one which was in fitting of his generational ideals. He was willing and eager to follow the Americans into war.

The baby boom political saga is to be told elsewhere. In Germany, Gerhard Schröder, a one time admirer of Blair, born 1944, won political office in 1998. Elsewhere, Nicolas Sarkozy became French President as late as 2007 (French presidential terms were seven years until the 2002 election). Sarkozy, while born just ten years after the second world war, perhaps identifies less with the baby boomer generation than those of his counterparts who were old enough to enjoy the summer of love. During the 2007 election campaign he railed against the 'soixante-huitards', that generation which rioted in the name of social revolution. For the would-be President the '68ers' were to blame for France's ills and their legacy should be 'liquidated' since it had elevated 'those who had said that anything goes; that authority, good manners and respect were out of fashion; that nothing was sacred, nothing admirable; that there were no rules and no standards; and that nothing was forbidden.'[9] This authoritarian streak is reflected in the French Burqa row. Plans to ban the wearing of the Muslim Burqa emerged from the French parliament (not a government initiative) in early 2010 and banned by overwhelming support by the July. And as *The Economist* argued: 'For American commentators who like to denounce European complacency in the face of an increasingly assertive Islam, France is an intriguing test-case... Liberal outsiders see this as intolerance. But to the French, who fought hard-won battles against authoritarian clericalism, and like America, it stems from a secular wish to keep religion in the private sphere.'[10] It is an interesting take on the mixed economic settlement where religion in the United States and Secularism in Europe have respectively developed over the period.

France and Germany led international opposition to the Bush/Blair invasion of Iraq but for no less selfish reasons. It was their own way of protecting riches and lifestyles. Iraq divided Europe perhaps because of their different experience of cold war. Military might was, after all, provided by the United States with Europe enjoying and promoting peace and prosperity. It was, after all, right on the doorstep of Western Europe. Germany and its capital city Berlin were physically separated. But the different experience and perhaps the pre-disposition to avoid military intervention did not mean the political leaders at the helm of these nations felt any less strongly about the ideological victory of the West over the East. Indeed the physical evidence of victory lay in the crumbled wall torn down in Berlin. And it is the differing experiences of these two great powers which unites and separates. Stephen Haseler's analysis of the New York terrorist attacks of 2001 is instructive: 'shared grief was not to be translated into a shared view of the world; for Europeans, the atrocity of 9/11 was not ultimately to become their own 'defining moment'. In Europe, in fact, 'everything had changed' some 12 years earlier. Europe's own seminal 'defining moment' was a different 9/11 – 9 November 1989.'[11]

Each seemed to mark a generational shift that told the world 'we are in charge now.' But the baby boomers coming to office in the West represented more than simply the handing over of power to a new generation though (as it perhaps had done briefly to J.F. Kennedy in 1960). It was about the cementing of our modern economic, political and social environment. But also a failure to develop and extend its power into a vision for the future. This generation limited our ambitions such as those futurologists of the 1950s might have enthused.

And while they were all about high ideals in rhetoric, they were the selfish ones. The baby boomers championed the mixed economic settlement and personified their near narcissistic generational attitudes. Growing and protecting our wealth at home and abroad was all well and good but its parochialism narrowed the destiny for all of us.

The Baby Boom Triumvirate Clinton, Blair, Bush

'We use the same toothpaste' George W. Bush told reporters through a proud smirk when asked what he and British Prime Minister Tony Blair had in common at his first visit to meet the new President. Despite personal and programmatic closeness to the outgoing President Clinton, Blair was determined to be at the front of the queue to meet his successor (and showed how close the settlement had brought politicians). There were many reasons to question the nature of this new 'special relationship' as ostensibly these were very different men. The Blairs and the Clintons, Tony, Bill, Hilary, Cherie, were lawyers; successful power couples. The two politicians had championed what became known as the third way to enable them to take their parties into office. They had relied on powerful media machines, focus group politics which came about as close to justifying Downs' rational choice models than any of their immediate predecessors.

Clinton, who had become one of America's youngest presidents, was into his second term by the time Blair's 'new dawn' saw Labour return to office for the first time in eighteen years. He served, consequently, as something of a father figure to the young Blair and the politics they jointly championed.

Bush was a quite different personality. His was, before 9/11, something of an isolationist approach to politics; a creature, it was said, of big business. His disinterest in foreign affairs and even the transatlantic relationship reflected his adopted Texan domestic ways. His lack of eloquence – straight talking as many would describe it – along with hanging chads and some neat legal manoeuvrings had helped him to grab the White House from opponent Vice President Gore (who attracted more votes). But this lack of sophistication was not seen as pertinent to building good relations with Blair who had been so close to Clinton, a veritable hate figure for many Republicans along with sections of the Democratic Party. Such hostility had a history which reached its pinnacle with the impeachment proceedings against Clinton, involved bitterness over his 1992 defeat of Bush senior and can be dated right back to the resignation of Nixon, of which a young Hilary had served as a member of the impeachment inquiry staff. Washington memories are long.

And woe betides any British politician who became entangled in this rivalry. Prime Minister John Major had allowed his Home Office to provide George Bush's 1992 re-election campaign access to their file on Bill Clinton's time at Oxford when he had expressed some opposition to war in Vietnam. Clinton's relations with Major in office were, therefore, frosty, ultimately having unfortunate consequences for the peace process in Northern Ireland as Sinn Fein leader Gerry Adams was all but legitimised, and prematurely, by the White House given the ongoing negotiations. Would Blair suffer a similar fate?

Pragmatic as ever, Blair picked up relations with Bush as rapidly as he had embodied the politics of the third way. But this was more than an adaptable politician. Blair spanned these two seemingly contrasting presidents because these baby boomers, different in personality, shared a generational perspective. And the practical consequences of this perspective was not, as is commonly observed, US led. Blair strained relations with Clinton in persuading him to intervene in conflict ridden Kosovo, even directly appealing to Americans on television. 'Why was I so keen to act? I saw it essentially as a moral issue. And that, in a sense, came to define my view on foreign and military intervention.[12]' Blair later recorded in his memoirs.

George W. Bush was born to be president in the sense that he was born into a political dynasty. His father was president and a significant public figure throughout his life. His grandfather, Prescott Bush was a Senator for Connecticut. But this Bush, a drinker and drug user, did not seem destined for greatness as a young big Bill Clinton had seemed to his contemporaries, despite his modest of backgrounds. But Bush, successively a one term governor of Texas and then president, was re-elected commander in chief in 2004. And with Blair in toe, Bush re-cast the way America projected its power on the world; putting into action the doctrine articulated by Blair. The shared view of the world, the certainty of their positions, meant that Bush-Blair in collaboration pushed the boundaries of this certainty beyond that possible by the Clinton-Blair relationship.

The context shaped by this unlikely triumvirate demonstrates a number of things. In an obvious way it shows the vacuity of the so called third way as little more than an electoral strategy for winning office. It shows that what links these politicians is a sense of their own 'right' combined with limited ideological baggage. But it is their generational shared view of the world which sits at the heart of these years which became so singularly focussed on protecting our great riches.

Cementing the Settlement

It is this generation of American and European politicians who are responsible for entrenching the mixed economic settlement into political life. While there are differences of emphasis in the USA and Europe, with Britain uncomfortably bridging the divide, from a distance their political programmes are ideologically consistent. Indeed, it is only with the end of the cold war and the shift in emphasis in the transatlantic relationship from security to more mundane matters of trade that small issues of contention have taken on an unwarranted significance[13].

It is notable that the political leaders who have helped to entrench the settlement in Western countries do not share party political traditions being spread across the so described centre left and right of their respective polities; representing Democrats and Republicans, Conservatives and Labour, CDU, SPD and the rest. And so, by the 1990s, Western governments had accepted each of these three conflicting forms of liberalism. And the first decade of the new century cemented each into the foundations of public policy.

In part, the broad idea was outlined in Francis Fukuyama's controversial 1992 book, *The End of History,*[14] in which the Johns Hopkins academic and *Reagan Doctrine* proponent, argued that as communism disintegrated across the world, Western liberal democracy represented 'the end point of mankind's ideological evolution'. With his US perspective and writing on the brink of the baby boom take-over, Fukuyama was celebrating the pragmatic acceptance of broadly open market economics and mass democracy. It is a case taken up by John Gray who argues:

> *The Soviet Collapse granted a new lease of life to the faltering American conviction that the United States embodies the modern age as no other country does. 'Declinism' –the perception that American power and prosperity are waning – was snuffed out. The world appeared to be converging on American values and institutions. Since then modernity, the free market and the universal reach of American Institutions have become virtually synonymous in the American public mind.*[15]

And even into the second decade of the twenty-first century there remains a 'broad, well-founded consensus about what constitutes good policy. No longer does economics lie.'[16] The reality is that the baby boomers who came of political age during a decade of remarkable peace and stability in the 1990s, used their time in office to cement the contradictory legacies of Attlee, Reagan and Dylan but without completing the project. That these ideas have been taken to be self-evidently correct, however, represents less the idea that history has ended than the demise in fresh political ideology during a long period of prosperity. After all, these politicians might have instinctively winced at one or other aspect of the settlement and yet it is their ideological inaction which it has to thank for its preservation.

Given that the political classes have long shown themselves to be rather liberal shy, the more pressing realities of economic hardship following the 2008 credit crunch could have seen the consensus put under pressure. It is an argument made by the Marxist philosopher, Slavoj Zizek who interpreted the terrorist attacks on New York in September 2001 as heralding 'an era in which new walls were seen as emerging everywhere',[17] and turning on the end of history thesis by way of these two seminal events of the first decade of the 2000s, has the dismissive opinion that 'Fukuyama's utopia of the 1990s had to die twice, since the collapse of the liberal-democratic political utopia on 9/11 did not affect the economic utopia of global market capitalism; if the 2008 financial meltdown has a historical meaning then, it is the end of the economic face of Fukuyama's dream.'[18] And yet it appears that the mixed economic settlement will survive. It might well undergo pragmatic change which while at close quarters could appear drastic, in the long sweep of retrospection will represent smooth consensus. Ideology would not seem to be returning to the instincts of the political elite even in the face of tremendous global financial pressures and geo-political change. And there does not appear to be anyone offering a coherent alternative or inclined to complete the mixed economic settlement project. It is this period and the years to follow which saw purpose dissipate in favour of response: powerful and confident responses to that which threatens our developed prosperity.

Tony Giddens, who for a time became the favourite academic theorist of Clinton and Blair, expressed the belief that the post 1989 world there was no real alternative and in doing so chimes with Fukuyama. The fact remains, that even if there were a coherent alternative, the developed world used the twenty years after the end of the cold war to grow and consolidate its riches. And those riches came to dominate the agenda as never before; even given the experience of the 1980s. It was Giddens who developed this reality into an academically respectable but party politically useful framework. In Britain and eventually across Europe, the approach was called the 'third way'; a meaningless political slogan which simply stood for the acceptance of mixed economy settlement.[19] A term which eventually (and rapidly) faded into disuse, it nonetheless served a generation of parties and leaders from the traditional centre left in the pursuit of open market economic policies. But it also obscured the need to offer an optimistic economic destiny.

Yesterday's Men and the Post-Baby Boomers

As our population ages, the obsession with youth is ever more acute. Just as our media is dominated by the fresh faced, so too is youth an increasing pre-requisite for political office. As the electorate itself grows older and more experienced, it seems the same is not a requirement for the great public office holders. To some extent President Obama personifies this trend in its most recent form. But whereas the youthful Bill Clinton chose a fellow baby boomer in Al Gore to be his 1992 running mate, despite the considerable experience of his incumbent opponent, Obama selected a man of his parents' generation in Vice President Joe Biden and, like Kennedy and Johnson before them, in doing so made a new generational contrast.

It is the baby boomers of the 1960s who perhaps see themselves as forever young, forever the children of the summer of love, who are increasingly dismissive of political figures of their own generation, demanding young leaders who speak of hope. And so, in just a few short years, that dominant baby boomer generation of politicians are becoming yesterday's men; replaced by the cohort of its political children. In some respects this is unsurprising since political candidatures tend to be about experience or change, and change is the more powerful slogan (trumped only by 'fear'). Biden himself was a candidate for the presidential nomination in 2007 and was forced into this very corner during a debate when he made the case (unsuccessfully) that the election 'is not about experience, it's not about change. It's about action.'[20] But it was Obama's inspiring demand 'for our generation to answer that call. For that is our unyielding faith - that in the face of impossible odds, people who love their country can change it'[21] which won the nomination and ultimately the presidency. But what does this generation stand for? And what will it mean for the mixed economic settlement?

Just as the post-war, cold-war, era with the great ideological battle between capitalism and communism was so fundamental to this now passing generation of politicians who accepted the mixed economy settlement and eroded wider purpose, the post-baby boomers' formative years have been dominated by technological change and the realities of rapid globalisation, the implications of which will be explored in a subsequent chapter. It is a contrast in experience, perhaps only just emerging, that once again, and so soon, is marking a shift in attitude. This new generational shift was analysed in an insightful 2008 article in *Newsweek* which surveyed democratic politics on both sides of the Atlantic:

To borrow a phrase from a previous era: there's something happening here. This new crop of politicians is different. Compared with the baby boomers, they are more technocratic, more global in outlook, more comfortable with technology, more idealistic and yet less ideological and less invested in old debates….

Many of these young politicos share a contempt for dogma—and an ability to find bridges between left and right. These are not veterans of the left-right battles that defined their parents' politics. Instead, part of their appeal lies in the sense that they have been able, and will continue, to upend the old order….

Ultimately, these new politicians may have a greater impact than those aging '68ers finally approaching their swan songs. They have made their entrances at a younger age, and so we will likely have them on the world stage for a very, very long time to come.[22]

It is debatable whether this cohort is really more idealistic even if it is clear they are less ideological. As Biden's slogan perhaps demonstrates, the idealism is shallow. This generation, while perhaps not as pragmatic as the argument might have them, are nonetheless driven by action and the strong motivation 'to do' on a global scale. Post ideological meant that the idealism became more focussed than ever on prosperity and while they expressed their hope of a 'fairer' future it was never more than a chalk stripe sideline to this priority.

The *Newsweek* article highlighted a number of prominent politicians in the United States and Europe who form this new generation. With Obama at the helm, British Foreign Secretary David Miliband, his fellow Cabinet colleague, brother Ed (and subsequently Labour party leader at just 40) and Conservative leader (and subsequently prime minister) David Cameron were cited alongside Fredrik Reinfeldt the Prime Minister of Sweden, Sarkozy protégé and French Justice Minister Rachida Dati, and Helle Thorning-Schmidt, leader of the Danish Social Democrats. This is the generation which grew up in and after the cultural revolution of the 1960s, a point which was not lost on 2008 presidential campaign watchers. Peter Canellos of the *Boston Globe* observed early on that 'Obama, who is 15 years younger than both Bush and [Hillary] Clinton, had the '60s in the rearview mirror during his formative years. He grew up in the aftermath of the huge cultural storm, not the middle. He saw a country engaged in the far less dramatic, but perhaps equally significant, endeavour of assimilating social changes'.[23]

Nowhere is this political-cultural shift more acute than in Britain where parties have become afraid to elect political leaders of an older generation. While his leadership style was left wanting and mannerisms old fashioned, Sir Menzies Campbell lasted but eighteen months as Liberal Democrat leader under a barrage of ageist media attacks on the then 66 year old during 2006-7.[24] As it became clear a general election would be more than two years away after Gordon Brown shied away from an autumn 2007 poll, Ming resigned to be replaced by the fresh faced, forty year old Nick Clegg (later to become deputy prime minister). The talented and experienced Vince

Cable ruled himself out of the contest on the grounds that he too was in his sixties.

Meanwhile, David Cameron's election to the leadership of the Conservative party at the age of 39 and with only one full term in Parliament behind him has become the political norm. After all, when he assumed the premiership in 2010, he was just 43, becoming the youngest PM in almost 200 years. Blair himself had been 43 in 1997 when he walked into Number 10, just a few months older than his 'heir'.[25] And it is a reality of politics which became apparent during the earlier Blair government but has since extended; this propensity toward not only the youthful, but also the inexperienced. The observation takes on real meaning when one recognises that the politician described as 'Heir to Blair' is not a Labour successor but rather a Conservative in David Cameron. For this is a generation of politicians who, across the mainstream political divide, share common characteristics. Aside from their youthful looks, good education and middle class backgrounds, these figures come into politics at an early age and without experience of the working world that most of us inhabit or have inhabited. Just look at the Labour leadership elections of 2010. The race to replace Gordon Brown was one crowded with identikit options of age, race, gender, background and experience. There were even two brothers in contention. It is little wonder that the then leading candidate (and elder brother), David Miliband, signed the black, woman, backbencher Dianne Abbott's nomination papers to join the race.

Typical today is to become an MP's researcher or adviser to a Minister or Shadow Minister or sometimes working for a think tank before scouting for a seat which is accessible as an insider. Once in Parliament, promotion is often rapid meaning few become accomplished Parliamentarians.[26] These people might be the 'brightest and the best' but their inexperience and minimal exposure to the life most people lead, the jobs they do and the problems they face raises questions about their ability to properly understand the needs of domestic policy. Their limited work experience outside of politics raises questions about their executive ability. And their attitudes make them more likely to pursue global rather than domestic aims. But it also means that these 'insiders' show little inclination to complete the mixed economic settlement project, broadening the vision of our capital's power and our potential destiny.

There are constitutional differences here too which have implications for executive ability and experience. The difference between a British style parliamentary (common across Europe) and an American executive presidential system is the make up of the Cabinet. Britain's is comprised of members of parliament with no background in their portfolio; people as much professional politicians as the PM. The US President, on the other hand, appoints his Cabinet from not only Washington politicians but industry and academia; people well suited to their briefs.

While youth is the attraction, a generational change in attitude is the result. And perhaps it is here that comparisons can begin to be made. David Cameron is a near perfect exemplifier of the political class. It is attitude rather than dogma that fuels policy positions and to an extent they represent the path of least resistance and in part they represent a shared journey of people and politicians; the direction of which was laid by the mixed economic settlement but it does not occur to them to lead us anywhere different.

In January 2010, on a slow news day, the British Social Attitudes Survey unexpectedly made the headlines. Over almost thirty years, Britons, it seemed, had become more socially liberal in terms of sexuality, in particular accepting of homosexuality, while their attitudes revealed a move to the economic right in terms of accepting inequalities.[27] For David Cameron, a patrician and pragmatic small and big 'c' conservative, such a popular mind-set could hardly be more convenient. No proponent of the cause, Cameron is nonetheless of a tolerant disposition and practical free market economic instincts sit comfortably with his beliefs. Obama is likewise tolerant in, for instance, his tacit support (though unwilling conviction) for gay marriage in the States but forthright in his promotion of prosperity. This generation has accepted the mixed economic settlement as entrenched.

Indeed in many ways, the post-baby boom generation is more comfortable with the mixed economic settlement as a package than the baby boomers themselves who were responsible for cementing it into public policy. This really is a post-ideological generation which knows little more than the political experience itself and are driven by this almost alone.

We have not seen the back of the baby boom generation. The 2010s have already seen former Presidents and Prime Ministers return to the world stage as envoys and special representatives. As life becomes tougher, solutions will be sought from all who are capable of making a contribution and these have now risen above petty politics to statesman standing. The baby boomers might well have left office but in other corners of society and policy discourse from academia to public services to law and diplomacy, this generation is at the top of the pile. And these baby boomers remain engrained

103

'statists' in their mindset and approach in a way that the post baby boomers do not. As it is the latter who today are leading government, it would seem that this attitudinal rift could be the cause of future friction in policy making.

Completing the Project

The post baby boomers eroded the policy differences between Europe and the United States and in completing the bequest of the baby boomer generation of political leaders, cemented the mixed economic settlement into public policy. Theirs is a pragmatism which, post ideologically, seeks to manage and tinker with the settlement rather than improve its philosophical approach or destiny. But it is this generation, in the second decade, which needs to complete the mixed economic settlement project that the baby boomers failed.

This project, which must be about what a rich society is for, will need to not only build consensus for difficult decisions but also be prepared to meet communities in partnership. It is ultimately a political strand which must challenge the cosy and artificial policy making at work today. And just as previous generations, in the 1930s and 1940s, made sacrifices for the future good of the world, this generation too needs to be prepared to be bold and altruistic. It is a challenge few appear motivated to accept. And, as the next chapter demonstrates, a host of factors have conspired to squeeze policy makers with a vice like grip.

Chapter Five

The Death of Domestic Policy

President Bill Clinton's rather quotable adviser James Carville once said that if he had another life he would 'come back as the bond market and intimidate everyone.'[1] It was a flippant remark but one which tells us a great deal about political decision making even in the United States, a country which under Clinton's leadership strode across the globe as the world's only superpower and which even subsequent developments have done little to undermine. The control that governments have over their domestic policy has long been exaggerated. The role of the state has changed and continues to change with a trend which has eroded the ability to alter radically the way we live our lives, certainly at election time.

This ideas has been tempered perhaps only by the (short-lived) assertion of more traditional authority in the wake of the global economic crisis. The limits on our policy have been brought about by the world we have created since the Second World War and have been broadly supportive of the mixed economic settlement but now raises questions about sustainability and indeed fairness in competing with new emerging economies on the very terms we have established. These limitations have also brought with them a malaise in confidence in traditional politics.

It is a myth that elections lead to frequent change in the big picture of policy. It is difficult to change policy in any dramatic way if one wants to and on the whole, politicians do not want to since they are conditioned by the settlements of their eras. Change in attitude, fresh approach and drive of a new administration can have positive (and negative) implications at least at the margins of policy and can make a difference to a variety of communities. But a dramatic philosophical shift in direction, driven predominantly by government, is elusive. It is the great events and great global changes which shift policy, shaping them for a generation of political leaders working within their confines, and with occasionally exceptional political leadership at their helm.

The mixed economic settlement came about because of the devastation of the Second World War, the cultural revolution and a dogmatic free market response to economic decline respectively. The collapse of communism by 1990 and the end of the cold war provided for the consolidation of these policies. And the deepening process of globalisation during the period has made the world ever more interdependent and reliant on common policy prescriptions. Similarly, the global economic crisis which began in earnest in 2008 has had perhaps the biggest impact since the collapse of the Berlin Wall on domestic and international policy alike. The consequences of actions taken by governments right across the world, a consensus personified by the delegates at the London G20 meeting in 2009, will shape policy for a decade, even if not as envisaged by those leaders at the time. Indeed, perhaps not in the controlled way which many proponents of the state predict. And, despite the rhetoric, policy in recovery was to be shaped by the two pragmatic forces of market confidence and fiscal necessity rather than as the result of any ideological commitment. It is a familiar story. This chapter discusses the impact of globalisation on politicians' abilities to form policy and shows how the changing world has elicited policy responses rather than leadership conforming to a narrow view with a permeating objective of protecting and promoting economic growth and our great riches.

The Limited Levers of Policy

Policy comes in all shapes and sizes and emerges from governments displaying different motivations and mandates. The rhetoric of political change and of hope expounds the idea that ambitions are limitless but the reality is that those pulling the levers of power in office find that there are fewer levers than expected and those that there are have a more muted impact than is popularly believed. Small measures can make a tremendous difference to people's lives at all levels of the income spectrum and not simply in a monetary sense. But when it comes to the areas of policy which matter most, those which change the way we experience life, society and the world, the levers really are few and largely inadequate. A relatively powerful political leader has the usual resources at his or her disposal.

There is tax and spending; interest rates and other monetary policies; there is legislation and the creation of offences; and (sometimes overlooked) there is the charismatic lever of diplomacy. At a simplistic level one might consider that if policymakers strip away everything they 'have to do', because of economic or social expediency, what is left? The answer goes some way to explain the elongated periods of pragmatic policy management experienced across the democratic world. But the response is more sophisticated than simply a dearth of dogma.

When policy is being formed or discussed, it tends to emerge in an atmosphere or at least using the language of rationality; it is self-evidently correct and can be implemented as such. Policy, though, is all too often (and not necessarily negatively) characterised by what Charles Lindblom has called 'disjointed incrementalism'. That is change will usually happen piecemeal, evolving and interacting with different interests and interest groups, some of whom will be highly resistant. As such, policymaking or at least policy implementation is concerned with bargaining, persuasion, delay, compromise and pluralism, emerging (incrementally) from established policy and political positions, making policy outcomes incremental also.[2] Incrementalists use budgets as a method of analysing trends and show that funding allocation is usually based on previous years' funding irrespective of policy flux. And a consequence of the economic success of the post-war developed world is that the trend of governmental budgets has been an expansionist one.

Nevertheless, incrementalism represents a position familiar to students of strategy who saw top down classical models tempered with evolutionary and processualist approaches which recognised the nature of competitive environments and cogitative political bargaining respectively.[3] For Michael Hayes, in his thoughtful analysis, the 'major drawback of policymaking in the United States is not that it is too incremental but that it departs from incrementalism too often, taking on a variety of pathological forms. If we want to make incrementalism work properly, we need more conflict not less.'[4] His rather sensible argument is that incrementalism is the superior form of policymaking since it is realistic about the limitations on policy and the nature of those with interests in the outcomes. Incrementalism has been criticised from all sides over the years – from the methodology to measurement to the lucidity[5] – and yet something in its simplistic and recognisable logic makes it an enduring model. There are alternatives, including models of 'punctuated equilibrium' which, drawing on biological observations, describe long periods of 'stasis' in policy, challenged by 'bursts' of radical change.[6] Such an observation is consistent with the idea of the mixed economic settlement where three bursts of change can be identified during a sixty year period. This does not mean, however, that the two models are mutually exclusive. Punctuated equilibrium explains policy in the broad sweep of history but it is incremental approaches which we experience most of the time and such experiences demonstrate the limitations of policy.

Policy can have both positive and negative effects on citizens' lives. But the truth is that the impact of badly formed policy will often be more deeply felt than the effects of good policy decisions. And the reason for this is the very limitations on policymaking in which this chapter is interested. To make successful policy is to be bound by those confines which limit. And notwithstanding extraordinary punctuated equilibrium moments, bad policy can represent sound intentions which conflict with external pressures. There are sound case studies in the Eurozone sovereign debt crisis and even less profligate economies where spending policies were brought to book by market pressures. We should not forget also that some policy is, of course, intrinsically poor and these very same case studies can be traced back to questionable decisions.

We can also get rather carried away with the idea that policy is just about what governments do or their intentions. Just as importantly is what they choose not to do. In any assessment of public policy this should not be overlooked.

In normal times then policy is inherently limited in what it can achieve. But such limitations go much further and in recent years much faster. There are huge demographic and social changes abound and there are moral hazards associated with some policy prescriptions which limit behaviour. And then there is the big issue of globalisation. The British Labour politician Ed Balls, as a young adviser on economic policy in 1994, coined a mouthful of a phrase: 'Neo-classical endogenous growth theory'. It never captured the public's imagination but what it meant was that politicians had to accept the state had minimal control over its economic destiny and should not attempt to make policy which would conflict with the power, ownership or place of capital. It is how administrations have governed during the decades of acceptance.

The World is Very Different Now

The period during which capitalism enjoyed its golden age and the legacy years of its wake have seen a transformation in the ways of our world. Reflected in wealth, demographic change, technology and the great power of corporations, these great shifts have an impact on our riches and our policy.

The years since the end of the Second World War have been witness to a huge population growth which has seen the number of humans walking on earth double to more than six billion. Indeed, there are as many people alive today as have ever lived before. While Europe and the States experienced its baby boom in the decade after 1945, birth rates have since dropped off.

The baby boom was followed by a 'baby crash'. In the EU, the average number of children per woman stands at just 1.5, projected to rise to just 1.6 by 2030, compared to the population replacement level of 2.1. Combined with increasing life expectancy during the post-war years, Europe, in common with the United States and other parts of the developed world, has an aging population, increasingly economically inactive and with more elderly people than ever before requiring healthcare and social protection.[7] Not so in the developing nations, especially Asia, where population explosion is located. There are projections which push world population to some ten and a half billion by 2050, with all of the growth coming from non-OECD developing countries.[8] These figures are accompanied by increasing urbanisation, something which is watched intensely by the United Nations' Population Division which reports some 3.3 billion of the world's population (more than half) habiting towns and cities, a trend which it forecasts will grow to almost 60% by 2030 and almost 70% by 2050. More people, living together in more crowded urban spaces, demanding housing, infrastructure and industrial growth. Following trends established during the industrial revolution, the world is becoming urbanised, putting pressures on societies in the developed West and developing East alike.[9]

With the population not only expanding but also greying the world is being shaped by the change. Life expectancy and birth rates mean that, in the West, there is an increasing strain on those in work as the baby boomers continue their charmed generational behaviour in retirement. Geoff Mulgan has argued 'Capitalist materialism has undermined the incentives for people to have children, sacrificing income and pleasure for the hard grind of family life. (And meritocracy further encourages parents to lavish their ambitions for advancement on just one or two children.) Hence the sharply reduced birth rates across Europe and among white Americans. At some point the resulting demographic imbalances threaten to undermine the generational contract which any society depends on, with a growing group of the elderly demanding ever more from a shrinking group of younger workers.'[10]

Meanwhile, there is evidence that baby boomers of the West have been 'reinventing old age'. As the first of this generation approached retirement age, the British think tank Demos published two fascinating and provocative accounts highlighting just how this most fortunate of people are not only wealthy in older age than their parents but are also in good health and exercise considerable power in their societies and countries. *The New Old* and *Eternal Youths*[11] respectively demonstrate the continuing reach of this generation in the story of our political economy with the latter arguing that it is not only the large (perhaps as much as 80%) percentage of financial assets which this generation controls but also the 'novel ways in which they will want to spend their money – and what they will expect in return'[12] including their lifestyles, impact on culture and infirmity. For Biggs et al, in their analysis of the trend, a 'striking characteristic of contemporary UK policy is a consistent attempt to drive down the age at which parts of the population are considered 'older', in a move to cast the discourse in terms of a "50 plus" life-course. So, while explicit reference to baby boomers is limited, UK policy has been marked by trends that push down the age of people affected by policies for "older people" such that it effectively includes this age cohort.'[13]

Combined with our accumulated riches, such dramatic changes limit and direct policy. The baby boomers are not simply the 'selfish generation', they are also more politically engaged. Across the democratic world, voter participation among the over 50s is significantly higher than those of the under 30s. Barak Obama was elected in 2008, in part by engaging the young and indeed, it is estimated that an extra 4 million under-30s voted in 2008 as compared to 2004 (itself an election which bucked the declining voting trend in this demographic – back in 1996 just 35% bothered to vote). But even here just 53% of the under 30s turned out,[14] compared to something approaching 67% of all voters. Combine this with the economic power of the over-50s, both in terms of income and capital and such a powerful constituency of interests cannot be overlooked by politicians. And here is the 'wicked problem' which afflicts policy making. Economically inactive baby boomers nonetheless create demands on policy and consume increasing resource as they age. Meanwhile, this economically and politically powerful demographic constrains the rebalancing of policymaking. This is the age group, for instance, which is least accepting of immigration, welfare (drawn by other people) and tax rises.

The other great development is that of technology which has become central to our lives and a great enabler to the way policy is directed but it is also fed by it. Joseph Schumpeter described how capitalism, fostering entrepreneurs, drives innovation and technological change; a gale of creative destruction (which would ultimately result in its own demise). And it is in capitalist markets that technology has advanced so very quickly. Technological determinism, a concept which has been extensively questioned, suggests that it is such development which now drives social and other change. We all experience this as technology determines the way we work, interact, communicate and live our lives. But it also leaves us with information overload meaning that some people are not as informed as they might be with less information. In such a world of knowledge, it is possible to witness a loss of authority and one can argue about the access to knowledge and the difference between the state and the citizen in this respect. It is reflected in the request by British Conservative Member of Parliament in August 2010 to have his name removed from a campaign website. Dominic Raab MP had said that the site 38 Degrees contributed to huge amounts of blanket emails which 'detracts time and effort'. Who has the knowledge or power? 38 Degrees response was to refuse to remove the address claiming it was in the public domain.

Nevertheless, technological determinism's most prominent contemporary proponent is Thomas Friedman, author of *The World is Flat*, whose often quoted argument draws technological advancement (and determinism) into the globalisation debate:

> *What I mean when I say that the world is flat is that sometime in the late 1990's a whole set of technologies and political events converged—including the fall of the Berlin Wall, the rise of the Internet, the diffusion of the Windows operating system, the creation of a global fiber-optic network, and the creation of interoperable*

> *software applications, which made it very easy for*
> *people all over the world to work together—that*
> *levelled the playing field. It created a global platform*
> *that allowed more people to plug and play, collaborate*
> *and compete, share knowledge and share work, than*
> *anything we have ever seen in the history of the*
> *world.*[15]

Such technological change has only sought to make the world smaller and further pressured policy into complying with the idea of the global marketplace and acting as a 'competition state'. Because while it might mean that opportunity is more equal, it also must mean that policy is more homogeneous. It is technology which enables the instantaneous information flow which supports global capital and facilitates its movement around the world as part of integrated markets. And it is technology which, in the growth of 'surveillance states', enables policy to protect our personal riches as well as providing an outlet for our insatiable consumer spending.

These big factors not only limit the ability of policymakers but they also dilute the effects of policy. Huge changes in demography, technology and culture influence the way things are done beyond the prescriptions of policy. And they tie into the changing demands of the harsh, global world.

The Tyranny of Global Markets

Taking a global view, the role of the state can be said to be shrinking. Year on year erosion has seen the public private balance tip steadily away from traditional state provision of goods and services to market provision. The period of history which saw the mixed economic settlement entrenched, has represented a relative decline of the public and corresponding growth of the private sector. Some countries, and Britain must be counted amongst their number, have seen the public sector expand in the years since Thatcherism and Reaganomics reigned. Some would argue unsustainably so. The trend, though, appears short lived and the post credit crunch pressures on public finances have provided a harsh check on spending.

Even with the cold war as a recent memory, Brian Martin argued that the place of the 'state and society in defining, protecting and promoting the public interest are being whittled away by a global campaign of privatisation and public sector commercialisation driven by the needs of transnational business'.[16] And in Mishra's view is the idea that neo-liberalism has now been transnationalised, limiting the ideological legroom in which policy can be made.[17] In practical terms this means that the traditional sovereignty of states and the elites which sit at the top of them is not only constrained, but the global nature of markets has forced countries themselves to restructure and co-operate internationally[18] which is part of the explanation for the growth of new public management in public services, in Britain especially since the advent of Thatcher.

Many of the most prominent writers on globalisation, including Karl Polanyi, see the trend as a near unstoppable force.[19] The implications for this change is a shift, as is identifiable in the evolution of the mixed economic settlement, from what Jessop describes as 'welfare states' to the more aggressive 'competition states' meaning that the focus moves from an inward, almost paternalistic, provision of services to improve the lives of its citizens (or as some would argue, to perpetuate the dependency of a portion of society), to paring down what the state does to ensure it can compete with other countries.[20] This competition has become all the more acute with the economic success stories of low cost nations emerging into economic strength in the East and elsewhere. The case against developed countries being complacent in this new world is very strong indeed. It was Lord Dahrendorf who argued that states were restructuring themselves to this end within the so called 'global marketplace'[21] and this schizophrenia can be seen in Europe in more recent years where the impetus has been to cut back on fat welfare states and generous employment rights in the face of competition from a rapidly growing and lean Chinese economy. And, as John Gray argues, there are implications for the nature of capitalism:

> *Gresham's law tells us that bad money drives out good. In a global free market there is a variation on Gresham's law: bad capitalism tends to drive out good. In any competition that is waged with the rules of global laissez-faire, that have been designed to reflect the American free market, the social market economies of Europe and Asia are at a systematic disadvantage. They have no future unless they can modernise themselves by deep and rapid reforms. Sovereign states are waging a war of competitive deregulation forced on them by the global market.*[22]

Gray, a British academic associated with both the new right of Thatcherism and the New Labour project of Tony Blair (and latterly a favourite of the Green movement) has been a fierce critic of how global neo-liberalism has played out, creating a certain 'social chaos' in the breakdown of community. But any protectionism against cheaper competition is surely unfair given that we created the rules by which these economies were forced to live. Such rational observations of the dangers inherent in the creation of riches on a global scale are even more worrying when they stem from the mainstream and indeed from the establishment. Former Chair of the Federal Reserve, Alan Greenspan offers a further warning (and did so before the economic crisis):

> *I have two grave concerns about our ability to preserve the momentum of the world's recent material progress. First is the emergence of increasing concentrations of income, which is a threat to the comity and stability of democratic societies. Such inequality may, I fear, spark a politically expedient but economically destructive backlash. The second is the impact of the inevitable slowdown in the process of globalization itself. This could reduce world growth and diminish the broad sanction of capitalism that evolved out of the demise of the Soviet Union.*[23]

The case he makes is that people feel deprived if the progress that expansion promised slows. It takes us back to the earlier analysis of our developed societies in which we compare our wealth to each other rather than the population of the wider world. Greenspan recognises this and acknowledges that 'capitalism' (in the terms that this book has discussed) 'now seems to be held in greater favour in the many parts of the developing world where growth is rapid... than where it originated, in slower-growing Western Europe.'[24] Global markets then not only play a large role in determining policy, but as the policy consensus of the developed, Western, world seeps into a global, free market consensus, the tragedy of our own riches has the potential to infect the world.

Who Wanted this Global Consensus?

The process of globalisation has been one of the great factors to have eroded the traditional power of the state. And it has done this as a consequence of both the pragmatic and dogmatic pursuit of riches as part of the mixed economic settlement. The fall of the Berlin Wall in 1989 was a seminal moment, not only for the millions who were to enjoy post-communist freedom in its wake, but also for the global balance of power. With the collapse of the Soviet Union and the end of the cold war, the United States of America was to become the world's sole super-power. And it achieved this elevated position at the end of a decade of radical, ideological upheaval domestically which had cast quite forcefully the market mantra into the mixed economic settlement.

This dogma was to weave its way into institutions domestic and international and is epitomised by John Williams' description of the 'Washington Consensus' in 1989 and what John Kay describes as being the American Business Model: an economic system with self-interest, market fundamentalism, minimal state and low non-redistributive taxes at its heart.[25] Combined, the Washington Consensus and the ABM can be seen as having been central to American power but the process of globalisation took that power beyond the borders even of the USA. The Washington Consensus was to become a by-word for this power of the intervening years. Williams was describing a so called 'consensus' among the world institutions which became based in Washington after the Second World War, and included the World Bank and International Monetary Fund, of policies to be pursued in developing economies, which at the time meant Latin America but has since broadened to include Africa, Asia and Eastern Europe. In that same year that saw the Berlin Wall raised to the ground, Williamson set out 10 macro-economic consensus undertakings of Fiscal discipline, Re-ordering public expenditure priorities, Tax reform, Liberalising interest rates, Competitive exchange rate, Trade liberalisation, Liberalised inward direct foreign investment, Privatisation, Deregulation (tariffs), Property rights.[26] John Gray puts the debate in stark terms:

> *The Washington Consensus assumes that the Hobbesian problem of maintaining order has been solved. It thereby not only pushes over the condition of the majority of humankind, which lives under enfeebled or collapsed states, it neglects the many ways in which unregulated world markets threaten cohesion in society and stability in government.*[27]

A decade on from his original observation, Williamson was critical of his term's application arguing that 'the phrase invited the interpretation that the liberalising economic reforms of the past two decades were imposed by Washington-based institutions like the World Bank, rather than having resulted from the process of intellectual convergence that I believe underlies them'.[28] There was certainly an ideological convergence, but not of a kind which was necessarily shared or controlled by the public, whether they live in the developed or the developing world and one which was focussed on a single strand of that mixed economic settlement.

The powerful idea of free, open, markets is at the heart of this consensus. As Gilpin argues, globalisation has brought huge advantages in terms of economic growth, but involves major externalities.[29] And has been seen to have been implemented in the interests of the institutions' backers our rich Western economies; though not necessarily Western government. After all, it can be argued that it has been the Washington institutions, not elected politicians, who have played the greater role of re-enforcing such dogmatic policies on those in power in Europe and the US, and imposed them on developing economies across the world. Indeed George Soros himself is of the view that the 'resource perspective' from which neo-liberalism operates is attractive not only to these international institutions, but also to governments.[30] It is here that Nobel Prize winning economist Joseph Stiglitz, became the biggest critic of Washington Consensus policies. In his pre-credit crunch book *Globalization and its Discontents,*[31] Stiglitz makes a forceful case as to how these institutions developed. Established under the Bretton Woods Conference (New Hampshire in 1944) a meeting which aimed to regulate post-war global monetary conditions, the International Monetary Fund and the World Bank were born. What were to become the Washington institutions were intended to support the Conference ambitions. World leaders agreed that 'nations should consult and agree on international monetary changes which affect each other. They should outlaw practices which are agreed to be harmful to world prosperity, and they should assist each other to overcome short-term exchange difficulties'.[32]

The British representative at Bretton Woods was the celebrated economist John Maynard Keynes and it is perhaps his influence which accounts for the tone of this summary; like a comparison with the visions of those futurologists, it is one quite foreign to the consensus which Williamson was to describe forty-five years later. Indeed, the international cooperation of the post-war world saw these Washington institutions pursue distinctly Keynsian, demand led, economic policy prescriptions for at least the first quarter century of their existence. Furthermore, Bretton Woods also pegged member countries' currencies to the US dollar which itself was pegged to the price of gold. Domestic policy making was therefore constrained and indeed shared as national Treasuries maintained their exchange rate in line with the dollar, re-or de-valuing only with the explicit agreement of the International Monetary Fund which itself was in a position to lend to member countries sufficient funds to smooth the effects of the economic cycle - all within the confines of the mechanism. Bretton Woods limited the domestic policy making as Keynes and US Treasury Secretary Harry Dexter White insisted on capital controls with the justification that only in this way could countries manage interest rates and achieve the policy priority of full employment.[33] But it was all nations whose domestic policy was constrained including the newly crowned economic superpower, the United States, where the Federal Reserve was bound to prevent dollar devaluation against gold and was a constraint agreed by governments not forced upon them by a faceless and unaccountable market.

The World Bank, on the other hand, was established to lend to developing countries and while commentators such as Will Hutton and Stiglitz speak broadly positively of these institutions' post-war record,[34] it is their later conduct that is criticised. For the consensus of the post-war world was gradually eroded and then abandoned, chiefly by the US in the early 1970s. President Nixon suspended the convertibility of the Dollar into gold in August 1971. 'The result was the emergence of greater capital mobility, floating exchanges and the creation of new financial instruments which were celebrated (until recently) by Alan Greenspan and Gordon Brown as the basis for economic prosperity.'[35] As a former chief economist at the World Bank, Joseph Stiglitz enjoyed a panoramic vantage point from which to observe the ideological, neo-liberal take-over of the IMF, World Bank and other bodies during the 1980s and 1990s, encouraged by the failures in Latin America.

This ideology (which showed little evidence of creating sustainable economic growth) saw the ABM imposed on the domestic policy making of developing economies to match those policies already adopted in the developed world.[36] To receive the much needed financial support, fledgling emerging economies have been required to privatise state services, open up their markets to powerful Western corporations and prematurely unlock their capital accounts, allowing for great capital flows which have destabilised and over-valued their currencies. From Latin America to Africa, policy has meant the American Business Model regardless of the widely held belief that such policies are inappropriate for early stage economic development.[37]

In the rich West we might imagine that we can be grateful that we do not suffer from the imposition of such policies. We would be wrong. What we describe as the Washington Consensus is surely more than a constraint on domestic policy making for countries rich or poor; it represents (or represented) the adoption of ideologically driven policies, largely irreversible by political will alone. Indeed, it took a shock of the magnitude of the post 2008 global economic crisis to undermine these ingrained policy prescriptions and even here the dogma proved impossible to dislodge.

Hazards Unsettled

Nassim Nicholas Taleb's book, *The Black Swan*, achieved a large degree of interest when it was published in 2007. Ostensibly it was about how financial markets misjudge risk and the consequent, catastrophic results of rare (black swan) events. It was about 'our blindness with respect to randomness, particularly the large deviations... [we] tend to see the pennies instead of the dollars... focussing on the minutiae, not the possible significant large events.'[38] But it also offered insights into risk-taking. A trader, say, is incentivised to make large profits; the pay-off of taking high risks on behalf of an investment bank's proprietary funds is potentially a very high personal bonus. But there is no commensurate incentive to be cautious. A trader who fails to grow his book will soon be out of a job and the penalty for a deal 'blowing up' is not personal financial liability but merely dismissal. The consequence is, therefore, greater risk taking. There is everything to gain from putting it all on the line, with very little to be lost by not taking the risk; the risk return trade off is distorted. Taleb's was a warning ahead of the banking crisis but it also offered a caution about public policy.

The economic concept of moral hazards assumed a new prominence for those observing the banking crisis. It is the idea that we naturally adjust our risk taking behaviour commensurate with the environment. Risk, in financial markets, policy or even in our life decisions, is not inherently a bad thing. There is a risk reward pay off that is all well and good so long as participants understand, accept and properly assess the risks involved in any venture. But the transfer of risk afforded by moral hazards distorts this equilibrium. As the banks teetered on the brink of collapse and the state stepped in to provide a kind of insurance required for the good of the system, they created a moral hazard that told the risk takers they need not bear responsibility for their actions. While the alternative for policy makers was the disintegration of the economic system, that very bail out meant the potential for greater risk taking in financial institutions since the risk was being transferred in turn from the banker to the bank to the government. It is a Hobson's choice for policy makers but it was not new.

In the early 1980s, the US Congress passed legislation which deregulated the Savings and Loan Associations but it decided to maintain deposit insurance which was state administered. What this meant was the creation of a moral hazard; the transfer of risk from the bankers who make the decisions to the state which would bail them out should things go wrong. Recklessness ensued leading to the 1989 Financial Institutions Reform, Recovery and Enforcement Act to restructure and re-regulate the industry. This author has set out elsewhere the idea of a *Regulatory Super-Cycle* where regulation follows excess and reduced public trust to be followed in turn by de-regulation after public confidence is restored but appetite for risk and return is deterred.[39] Together they illustrate the limitations of policymaking and the unintended incentives. Such incentives can be seen elsewhere: in what some have described as the 'blackmail' by big business and corporations to relocate were taxes to rise beyond that which they feel are acceptable, for smaller businesses to create jobs, to educate and to train; for people to ensure self-sufficiency, save for retirement or rely on the state. Policies can incentivise and often with unintended consequences. It all limits policy-making.

Joseph Stiglitz

One of the reasons that Joseph Stigliz's damning critique of globalisation enjoyed great attention was that it emerged from such an insider. Stiglitz is one of the gilded few to have received a Nobel prize for economics, awarded for his work on asymmetric information, imperfect markets and consequent market failure. He was Chief Economist at the World Bank from which vantage point he watched his fears unfold and where his own dissent eventually led to his departure. 'I saw firsthand the devastating effect that globalization can have on developing countries, and especially the poor within those countries.'[40] Stiglitz was Chairman of President Clinton's Council of Economic Advisers, near the very centre of policy making.

A prolific writer, he has always been able to disseminate his views which, given his onetime insider status, are all the more powerful. There are dozens of well known critics of capitalism to have gained notoriety, in particular since the late 1990s when anti-globalisation protests coincided with Stigliz's term at the World Bank. But Stiglitz stands out in his condemnation of globalisation and 'neo-liberal economics' because of that impressive CV. And it is his 2001 book, *Globalization and its Discontents*, which made his name beyond the academic community or public administrators. Its front cover proudly announces the million plus copies sold; each reader absorbing the powerful, if sometimes self-indulgent, prose.

A renegade economist and detractor of the Washington institutions which exercise such power over public policy, he is nonetheless (or consequently) an attractive figure to politicians. President Obama even brought him back in to advise on economic policy. But this did not prevent him from delivering an outspoken criticism of the young administration's attempts to tackle the financial crisis: 'All the ingredients they have so far are weak, and there are several missing ingredients... The people who designed the plans are either in the pocket of the banks or they're incompetent.'[41] With friends like these...

The Brief Return of the State

The International Monetary Fund estimated that banks in the U.S. and Europe lost more than $1 trillion on the so-called 'toxic assets', a figure estimated to top $2.8 trillion from 2007-10 as banks across the world were bailed out by governments who pumped billions of dollars into the system and in some instances took equity shares. The most dramatic and the peak of the crisis came with the collapse of giant investment bank

Lehman Brothers in October 2008, despite pleas to George Bush's White House to step in. Placing the crisis firmly and singularly at the feet of anonymous bankers, a group of people who became universally vilified during and after the crisis might be good politics, but it is poor economics and even worse history.

The actions of the banks were central to the crash but they did not act alone. Public policy was to blame to some degree for the meltdown as was the consequence of that process of globalisation which created a global pool of money roaming the globe in search of the best returns. There was a collective failure of regulation, low capital adequacy requirements across the world and economic policies which created and sustained a housing boom. This included the so called 'Greenspan put' which saw the Federal Reserve maintain interest rates at historic lows for the early part of the young century.

In Britain, as Chancellor, Gordon Brown is surely implicated in the years up until the crash and there is an important connection to public services. With fifteen years of uninterrupted growth in his train, Brown believed he had ended boom and bust. And the Blair government in which he dominated had an ambitious plan to increase dramatically spending on public services. An accusation of Brown made by Polly Toynbee is that he tried to build a Swedish welfare democracy on US levels of taxation. It borrowed when it should have made the case for taxation and at a time of low interest rates 'floated on air'. The City of London with its financial services sector was a cash cow which financed public sector spending over many years and to keep London attractive, Ministers boasted that Britain's regulation was even lighter touch than the US. It is said that the Treasury pressurised the Financial Services Authority into leaving certain financial institutions alone. In hindsight, there was an inevitability about the crisis. But, it should not be forgotten, that with a free market funding the public sector, the period saw the mixed economic settlement maintained.

But it is the response of the state and the implications for policy which are of central importance. Once the crisis struck, cherished economic policy was all but abandoned almost overnight and governments across the world intervened in the economy and in the banking system like never before. An early victim of the crisis was the British high street bank Northern Rock which had over-leveraged its positions, requiring Bank of England support which in turn led to queues of panic-stricken savers demanding withdrawal of their money. The state stepped in and nationalised it. The Royal Bank of Scotland followed. But RBS is more than a high street bank. It is a global investment institution which, at its peak, was the fifth largest bank and the tenth largest company in the world, employing some 170,000 people. And the British state was to acquire upwards of 70% of its shares (rising to more than 80%). The government fed some £37bn into RBS alone which is more than a third as much as it spends on the entire NHS each year. And as part of a £500bn rescue package some 40% of a newly formed Lloyds TSB-HBOS fell into state hands. In the United States, the government stepped in to manage the Federal Home Loan Mortgage Corporation, the Federal National Mortgage Association, Fannie Mae, Freddie Mac and Citigroup. Ireland, Iceland and The Netherlands followed. And while the so-called 'Anglo-Saxon model' was criticised by more statist Western Europe, let it not be forgotten that

German, state controlled, regional banks were found neck deep in the toxicity.

For Britain, and with an eye on the mixed economic settlement, this was the biggest nationalisation programme since Attlee's 1945-51 government and in real terms might even be more expensive. The state effectively grew with its once timid tentacles reaching as far as international banking. Years of the market knows best ideology was seemingly abandoned in favour of old fashioned post-war consensus, pragmatic Keynesianism. And this was mirrored by the sort of international co-operation of that era too. The G20 rapidly became the forum for decision making and co-ordination (not the narrow G8) and governments across the world recapitalised the banks, loosened fiscal policy and injected billions of dollars, euros, pounds, yen, renimbi and the rest into the global economy.

The events since the banks went into meltdown have led numerous analysts to re-assess the direction of state power. Dryzek and Dunleavy, for instance, in a detailed examination of the state, its development and theories of its operation, could not help but highlight newly discovered confidence in the state in marketing their comprehensively considered book.[42] Many self styled 'social democratic' writers celebrated this change in public policy; a gleeful smile towards action which seemed to eschew liberal market fundamentalism, the Washington Consensus. Instead it reasserted state control, state power and state influence in our economies and over domestic and international policy alike. One such writer was the former German Minister for Economic Co-operation, Erhard Eppler. In his book *Return of the State?* (notable perhaps for the astute inclusion of a question mark) Eppler celebrates the fact that in an economic crisis which rivalled the great depression, it was the long shunned state that was turned to save the banks and to rescue the economy. In the 2009 epilogue to his 2005 publication, he riles:

> *Amidst the current flurry of bank nationalisations and government bail-outs across the world, a common theme is emerging: it is the state, so stridently written off for so long by so many, that it is now having to intervene to prevent financial markets and reckless bankers from ruining the world economy. Even in America, the heartland of the neoliberals and neoconservatives, it is the state which is now stepping in to shore up the banking system and restore confidence in the markets.*[43]

He might be right to an extent. The state did reassert itself, the markets appeared to be tamed and the Washington institutions were not only humbled by their seeming failure but they have also been undermined by a new influence demanded by the China led East. The new role of China and the growing realisation that this mighty nation would demand influence and voting rights on international organisations more fitting to its global prominence is an abiding feature of the crisis. Despite being the world's second biggest national economy worth some $8 trillion and representing some 20% of the population, at the time of the credit crunch its voting share on the IMF and World Bank represents just 3.66% and 2.78% respectively compared to the United States 16.77%/16.38% and the EU's 27 members' combined 32.08%/28.55%.[44] One potentially significant consequence of global economic meltdown over the coming years could be a real shake-up of these Washington based institutions which exert huge power and influence over the world economy.

Alas, while the state briefly reasserted its authority, there was nothing philosophical about intervention or nationalisation. Indeed as the grimace on the face of former US Treasury Secretary Hank Paulson was testament, some of it was done through gritted teeth (indeed there was even a report that he was physically sick). Governments showed themselves to be rather desperate to return the banks to the private sector. And, in contrast to earlier nationalisations, it is very difficult to argue that the likes of the Royal Bank of Scotland became public service or its 170,000 employees were civil servants. Indeed, save for pressurising them to lend to British business (which probably contravened trade rules), the state avoided getting involved in how these banks are run despite widespread concerns.

And the huge cost of bail-out, fiscal stimulus, tax cuts and the usual cost of downturn mean that public finances in places such as Britain, the United States and numerous Eurozone countries emerged from recession in a dire state. As economies returned to growth, anaemic as it was, it was payback time for the countries who had 'saved the world' and for the people who had been saved. In bailing out the system, in recovery global markets re-established their power and once again forced a homogony of policy. Ironically, the G20 meeting in April 2009 represented a political consensus among the leaders involved. By Toronto in 2010, leaders agreed to pursue their own countries' agendas but that meant acquiescing to the demands of global markets. President Obama's plea to Europe not to prematurely cut spending was, after all, drowned out by the howl from the bond markets demanding that national treasuries bring sovereign debt under control.

Britain entered the financial crisis with a relatively low (by EU standards) level of public debt of around 40% of GDP and a relatively small budget deficit. It struggled into recovery with national debt peaking at a whopping 80% of GDP and a deficit rising to £175bn or 12.4% of GDP. Giving evidence to the Treasury Select Committee, in November 2009, Bank Governor Mervyn King impressed the need for a 'significant reduction in borrowing over the lifetime of the next parliament to eliminate a large part of the structural deficit'.[45] Furthermore, The Fiscal Responsibility Bill which was announced in the Queen's Speech around that time provided for a statutory basis for reining in the deficit and debt, halving it within four years. And the incoming coalition government of 2010, pleased markets (evidenced by an appreciation in Sterling) by savagely cutting back on public services, spending and just what it is that the state does. Chancellor George Osborne pledged to eradicate the UK's deficit within a Parliament and by 2011 there had been angry protests on the streets about the harshness of cuts.

It is an issue which was shared by countries across the globe and as a debt crisis erupted in the Eurozone markets once again pressured governments to bring spending under control lest they force them to become 'uncompetitive states'. The so-called PIGS countries of Portugal, Italy, (Ireland), Greece and Spain, drawn together in this somewhat offensive acronym (Barcap's analysts were banned from its use), ran up such huge national debt as to destabilise the Eurozone and raise questions about the future of the single currency itself. In a necessary effort to prevent global markets from destroying the credibility of the Euro, it was once again the German taxpayer who stepped in to rescue these economies.

It leads to a near inevitable new stage in global policy. The second decade seems set to prioritise sound public finances, trade balancing and reduced borrowing. Domestic policy makers will be required to acquiesce to these terms imposed by a global system of which we are all part.

The ultimate consequence of massive intervention is surely that the celebration of the newly found power of the state was a short-lived and over optimistic one. Once economies were stabilised, it was business as usual: manageable debt and a policy of growth. The markets had won. The return of the state has rapidly been replaced by nations prioritising their finances and searching for opportunities to divest responsibility for public services. President Obama's healthcare reforms fly somewhat in opposition to this argument of state demise. But even with some Republican opponents expressing the view that 'this is the state muscling in' on services which should be the preserve of the private system, such ideologically opposition can usually be found on the momentous side of the trend, promoting an almost singular spotlight on expansion. And where economic growth is key could we see a return of the arguments over being competitive states and competing with China?

The Limits of Policy

Economic policy can be said to be the umbrella of all other policymaking. And in our developed as well as developing nations, economic policy is determined by global markets to a far greater degree than our politicians are often willing to acknowledge. Globalisation has been successful at creating riches, low inflation, consumerism and has helped to pay for public services. In doing this it has also helped to maintain the mixed economic settlement and to some degree prevented further progress. It is the mighty global markets, too, which punish economies whose policymaking steps out of line. And with capital so mobile, information so free and technology-based systems so abundant, that capital moves very quickly indeed. Where we might have expected a political strand to the settlement, politicians have allowed mighty markets to fill the void. The dogma of the Washington institutions might have been good for the West during the decades of acceptance, but the levelling of economic conditions has only sought to limit policy choice. Those markets, humbled as they were by the credit crunch, banking crisis and global recession, should not be expected to express gratitude for government bail-out. The state might have staged a brief return, but it was not long before the markets reasserted their power.

But there is another reason why our governments have shown timidity in redressing such limits. The baby boomers in office not only allowed our ambitions to be limited but also perpetuated a 'have it both ways' cheat at the heart of politics which has become unsustainable.

Chapter Six

The Unsustainable Cheat

Ronald Reagan, in his day, perhaps came to epitomise the unsustainable cheat at the heart of contemporary governance. A great flaw in democracy is the reconciliation of conflicting demands. In a sense, democracy is about managing these demands; it is one of its great strengths. And in the mixed economic settlement, forged in the memory of hot and cold war, trying to reconcile these demands peacefully served only to demonstrate the superiority of Western politics. But it has its flaws. Post ideological democracy requires of politicians that they meet both sides of these competing demands. Politicians are told to cut taxes whilst increasing spending; to reduce global warming but to encourage economic growth; to take decisions for the long-term but be judged in the short. It is a tragedy of our riches which is far worse today than when Reagan occupied the White House.

Back in 1981 President Reagan sat outside his California ranch, replete in cowboy denims and boots, and before a throng of press reporters, photographers and camera crews signed into law the Economic Recovery Tax Act. With questionable ideological momentum (and reliant on the Laffer curve's

fortuity), the ERTA was a plan to stimulate economic growth by slashing tax, especially for the richest. Reaganites were attracted to the theories of Professor Arthur Laffer who proposed the idea that where taxation is set very low, no-one seeks to avoid it and where it is set very high very many people avoid paying. Reducing taxation, he suggested, increases revenues. The evidence of ERTA's effectiveness is mixed to say the least, having an impact on 'excessive' but minimal impact on more static rates. There was evidence for this at the time with analysis drawing on historical comparisons with the 1920s and 1960s when similar policies were enacted.[1] But it was a convenient story, a cheat that said you can have the same amount of revenue and spending but on lower levels of taxation. It is a cheat in which politicians and public alike were content to collude for the outcome was the protection and promotion of our riches. ERTA is a singular example of the unsustainable cheat at the heart of democratic politics. But today's 'cheats' are more unsustainable than ever. Reagan was an ideologically driven politician who was able to govern by achieving a bare majority but a majority of fellow travellers. Divide and rule politics died during those decades of acceptance and today's politics is more difficult than ever.

Despite, or indeed because of, our societal riches we have become increasingly complacent about democracy and wilfully ignorant of many of the issues beyond the basic maintenance and promotion of our standards of living. We should perhaps not kid ourselves that this is a new issue, though the six decades since Frank Knight wrote the following have made the situation all the more stark: 'Electors educated in and by democracy tend to combine lack of respect for "politicians" with the belief that elected officials will satisfy any craving by

138

fiat, if only the right pressure is brought to bear.'[2] If politics is going to be the strand which completes the project of the mixed economic settlement, we need to understand what has become of democratic discourse in our contemporary system.

There is an episode of *The Simpsons* where, led by an angry Homer, the citizens of Springfield demand that Mayor Quimby provide a new, though unnecessary, 'bear patrol' following the incidence of a bear being captured in town but then equally angrily refuse to pay for it. The result is a scapegoat 'Proposition 24', a referendum on immigration.[3] It captures our politics satirically and magnificently. Our standard of living, in monetary terms, is such that most people are largely disengaged from their political system and do not invest of themselves in their democracy. Our societies take our riches for granted just as they are complacent about their democracies. The shocking truth is that our democracy is far more fragile than we might imagine.

We might look around the world and see democracy safeguarding our wealth but as John Keane's excellent history points out, in 1941 there were just eleven functioning democracies in the world. That will not stop electorates from punishing politicians at the ballot box where riches are put in peril and punishing them just the same where they do not deliver on conflicting demands. Tribal party politics and the fiction of left and right ensure that while there is continuity of action in office, there is no political collectivism on most of the big and difficult issues of the twenty first century. We cling to these outdated descriptions of left and of right but they prevent us from dealing with the essential issues which now need new and innovative partnerships if they are to work. And yet there remains the unspoken consensus on the mixed economic settlement. Reagan might have perpetuated the cheat but he did so pursuing a dogma; today it is practical politics. We are all implicated in the decline in politics but the cheat has become unsustainable. The party system as we now know it is part of the problem. Politics needs to be refreshed if there is to be any hope of offering a more optimistic future. Both Quimby and Homer are wrong.

Inconsistent Demands, Flawed Promises

There is heuristic value to Anthony Downs' 1957 political science classic, *An Economic Theory of Democracy*. He proposed the idea of voter and politician as rational actors; the former seeking to maximise pleasure, the latter to maximise votes.[4] As a starting point, it provides food for thought that office seeking political parties are simply offering the electorate what they think it wants. It is a concept which has been discussed at length elsewhere, by this author amongst others,[5] and is a flawed proposition not least because it does not stand up to historical interpretation.

Furthermore, as Dunleavy argues: 'It is not feasible to hold both part of Downs' model at the same time. If governmental or state power has the extraordinary significance described by Downs, it will confer on the party of government the ability to shape aggregate distribution of preferences in the electorate and indeed to change individual voters' preferences'.[6] That is the power of office is the commensurate power to shape preferences. And we see this in everyday campaigning of democratic party politics. But while Downs' lacks the sophistication of the reality of political choice, in particular given the punctuated periods of philosophical policymaking, it shows that electoral demands must be addressed by politicians seeking election. Downs overlooks the importance of ideology. Today we might be post ideological but that does not mean politicians have no conviction about a course of action – just ask George Bush and Tony Blair. It is just that in the thrust of policy mainstream, there is a great deal of tacit agreement. The problem too for the politician is that we create wicked problems demanding our cake and insisting on eating it. It is what the great American poet Walt Whitman described as 'an American problem' in his 1892 prose works: 'how to combine one's duty and policy as a member of associations, societies, brotherhoods or what not, and one's obligations to the State and Nation…, the true nobility and satisfaction of a man consist in his thinking and acting for himself. The problem, I say, is to combine the two, so as not to ignore either'.

In our rich societies, we want it all. But some of our wants conflict and are mutually exclusive. And so, we want them now. Democratic politics with its three, four or five year terms in office are quite naturally short-term. Readers will recognise the nature if not the specifics of the following examples of political discourse.

The most famous Governor in the United States in recent years has surely been Arnold Schwarzenegger of California. The 'Governator' ousted incumbent Gray Davis during a 2003 recall election in a piece of pure political glitz and theatre befitting of tinsel town itself but which bore little relation to the great issues of the day. California politics is a living history of our contradictory demands with its wonderfully entrenched 'propositions'. Davis had a zeal for education and during his first term, with popular support, spent billions of

141

extra dollars on education. In fact he spent $8 billion more during his first term than was required of him by the California constitution. Proposition 98, adopted in 1988, requires Governors to spend at a minimum and growing amount on education each year and represented a challenge to the 1978 proposition 13 which limited the amount Governors can raise in property taxation and state tax rates. Enshrined into law, requiring a two thirds majority to amend, is the requirement to both increase spending and control taxation.

Germany is a country which has survived deindustrialisation of the 1980s with a significant amount of manufacturing and engineering intact and has clung on to a notably generous employment rights and state sponsored social insurances. German workers are, consequently, amongst the most expensive in the world. Maintaining such a sector has not been easy and jobs have seeped out of the country to lower cost economies of the East. For many in government, the answer was to be a rather pragmatic (not Thatcherite ideological) process of deregulation for those running businesses and of labour laws. While Angela Merkel's governments have had high ideals of pushing through such reform, the electorate has been stubbornly of the view that it expects to maintain its jobs and the expensive social protections that go with them.

France has one of the highest life expectancies in the world and, just like the rest of Europe, a rapidly aging population. In September 2010 there were full scale strikes across Paris. Transport workers were joined by postal deliverers, teachers and other civil servants united in protest against President Sarkozy's plans to raise the retirement age from as low as 55 for some public sector workers to over 60. The opposition, hypocritically, was quick to lend its support even despite the status quo being a clear unsustainable cheat.

The pressures can sometimes be resisted, however. Newly elected, Britain's coalition government restored the link between pensions and earnings in its first Budget in 2010 (rather than up rated with inflation as had happened since the 1980s). It was a grand gesture which in some respects was overdue, in other respects fitted in to a reappraisal of future retirement, and in yet another respect was relatively inexpensive in the short-term at least. Contrast this, for instance, with the pressure building on the then Chancellor to re-link pensions to earnings, during the 2000 conference season. As inflation figures were published, it was calculated and widely publicised that the indexed rise in pensions would be £2.25 per week. To re-link to earnings would cost just £2.65 per week, easily affordable; especially at the time with the economy healthy and accounts in surplus. But while the decision would be easy in the short term, it was projected that by 2050, the cost to the taxpayer would have grown to some £100bn per year, compared to £55bn if the rise remained linked to inflation. Government took an uncharacteristically unpopular decision, in the long term good of the country. It would gain no electoral advantage but the circumstances were such that the government was politically comfortable.

Earlier that year though, the contradicting demands of the electorate did make government change its policies. Public pressure became so intense that Prime Minister Tony Blair was forced to announce increased spending on the NHS impromptu during a television interview with David Frost.[7] His announcement caused considerable friction with his Chancellor where relations were already fraught. But nevertheless, the commitment to spend as much as the EU average became policy. Did this satisfy the electorate? It was just a few months later that angry protests over the level of fuel tax brought much of the country to standstill. More spending and less taxation please. And by the way, we would like to be able to pollute at will but have clean air. These are the 'wicked problems'. In their own way sometimes trivial but there is a much bigger one where so much more is at stake.

Costing the Earth

Two big international summits took place in 2009. The first, in London in April, saw a meeting of the G20 which met to agree a package of measures aimed at returning the global economy to growth. The second, in Copenhagen in December tried to reach agreement on tackling climate change. That Copenhagen was an unmitigated disaster while London pumped billions of dollars into the economy demonstrates not only conflicting priorities but is also testament to the overarching demand that our riches are protected. It shows also our conflicting demands. The Copenhagen summit produced an optimistically phrased Accord which opened:

> *We underline that climate change is one of the greatest challenges of our time. We emphasise our strong political will to urgently combat climate change in accordance with the principle of common but differentiated responsibilities and respective capabilities... We recognize the critical impacts of climate change and the potential impacts of response measures on countries particularly vulnerable to its*

adverse effects and stress the need to establish a comprehensive adaptation programme including international support.[8]

While this document managed to draw signatures from across the world and included those from the USA and China, the biggest polluters, it failed to illicit any legally binding targets. Furthermore, the conference only agreed to 'take note' of the Accord rather than adopting its contents enthusiastically. The Accord was brokered by President Obama, encouragingly progressive in comparison with his predecessor. Alas the conference missed an historic opportunity to deal with a crisis which threatens the very survival of our planet. There was no such opportunity missed in London to deal with the economic crisis which threatened the survival of our riches. Here world leaders did not simply 'take note' of the need to kick start the global economy, they enthusiastically rescued the banking sector and pumped billions into the system

The case for tackling carbon emissions, climate change and environmental destruction has been made forcefully in academic, political and activist circles alike and consequently does not need to be rehearsed here. But what is true is that economic growth has historically been incompatible with environmental protection. This is a sweeping statement that, naturally, requires qualification, but nonetheless has a fundamental truth at its core. According to the International Energy Agency, greenhouse gas emissions fell during 2009 by around 3% and some three quarters of this reduction can be attributed directly to the reduction in industrial activity resulting from global recession.[9] That is to say that one of the most effective checks on climate change has been slowing and negative growth, not targeted policy outcomes. We demand of our political leaders conflicting policy positions: we demand that they cut greenhouse gasses but will punish them at the ballot box if they take away our cheap air travel. We send them off to negotiate climate deals but require those same world leaders to get together to further trade and growth.

It will come as little surprise that the richest consume and pollute the most. The richest 500 million people on Earth are responsible for near 90% of consumption and half of all global CO_2 emissions.[10] Any substantial change in emissions, therefore, requires a substantial change in the behaviour of these people. But not only them. Industrialising nations such as China perceive a threat to the potential economic wealth they can create, a potential likely to be checked by curbs on emissions. Irrespective of the environmental crisis, the protection and development of our riches trump our desire to collectively tackle the issue. The process of global negotiations aimed at protecting the environment have consequently been less about cutting omissions than countries 'getting a good deal'. This was highlighted at the Bonn summit in June 2010 when Bolivia delivered a paper showing that the outcome has been that rich countries could actually pollute more. It was more about protecting wealth creation than it was about protecting the environment.

Giddings, Hopwood and O'Brien address some of these issues by demonstrating that so-called 'sustainable development' is often categorised as reconciling the competing demands expressed in the concentric rings of environment, economy and society. They highlight the limitations of such models and argue:

The reality of life today is that the economy dominates environment and society. The large global companies dominate decision making, including that of many governments. Also international forums and organizations, heavily influenced by the large corporations, take decisions without even the modest level of democratic control that exists on national governments. Whilst central government and business have embraced sustainable development, the separation into the three sectors can be used to justify a concentration on a part, rather that the whole. In most cases, governments' main concern is economic growth.[11]

Their case, that these divisions only serve to hamper the cause of sustainable development, is compelling as is their call for us to stop seeing our actions as compartmentalised. This book will address some of the practical reconciliations in a later chapter but for here, the point has been made that a tragedy of our riches is the failure to reconcile the demands of wealth creation and protection of the environment through a politics created to sustain our riches.

More Wealth Means More Wants

The richer we have become, the more confident we are in our demands. One feeds the other but those demands stretch further than our private consumer and material demands for goods and services; the glittering and the shiny goods in shop windows, holidays in sunny climes, wondrous food and drink from home and abroad. As we have enjoyed greater choice of this kind, we too have demanded or at least expect greater choice and diversity in our public services. A permanent loss of output, as experienced as a result of the credit crunch, however, does not mean that we will be any more accepting of cuts in services. By 2011 public spending cuts in Britain had led to protests on the streets. Students, trade unions and motorists combined to call for the maintenance of spending and (separately) demands for lower fuel duty. Meanwhile polls showed broad public agreement with the need to cut the deficit. Similar protests took place in France, Belgium, Spain and Greece.

Choice is a near universally popular concept. Who wants less choice? And the mixed economic settlement has delivered increasing choice in private and public spheres alongside greater wealth over the decades of acceptance. Choice demands excess capacity of course and in a period where we are marginally poorer, would our political system allow for such unpalatable demands to be reconciled?

There's More to Life than Left and Right

During the French Revolution, liberal deputies from the Third Estate, working people and the bourgeoisie, would sit to the left of the president's chair; members of the Second Estate, the nobility, would sit on the right. Hence the terms left-wing and right-wing were born. Terms which bear little resemblance to the way they are used today and indeed, the way those terms are used today differs from the way they were used even just a generation ago. Post ideology, left and right have become little more than a refuge for both politicians and the electorate; *an ivy which covers a political trunk*, if you like. They are easy identifiers which permit our selfishness behind a veneer of principle. But as parties have shed their distinct beliefs, are left and right terms any more meaningful than simple marketing? Or worse, because they support dysfunctional, even hypocritical politics they justify the cheat and prevent us from properly addressing issues such as these. The baby boomers and the post baby boom generation have happily employed the cover of left and right yet their actions can be seen as broadly ideologically consistent.

The French Revolution, of course, resulted in the downfall of absolute monarchy and could not be said to have been the finest hour for French nobility. The brutal reality of this key episode in European history has left a long and deep impression on French culture. Perhaps this is why, even today, regardless of objectivity, mainstream French politicians so often consider themselves to be of the left. Similarly, in the United States, the paranoid legacy of Senator Joseph McCarthy's hunt for Communist sympathisers during the 1950s and that post-war suspicion of collectivism, has meant that few aspiring political candidates describe themselves as 'liberal' let alone 'left wing' and certainly never 'socialist'. In Britain, the impact of Margaret Thatcher and her part in the mixed economic settlement shifted debate so decisively by the end of the 1980s that voices once considered the moderate centre-left latterly replaced extreme left-wingers who seemed to have all but disappeared. The decade long Blair government, continued to be described as 'left-of-centre' for no other reason than the inheritance of the century of Labour politics from which it took power. Meanwhile, governments of both 'left' and' right' descriptions suppress liberties, freedoms and democracy and pursue, single-mindedly, the generation of wealth. Where the priority is the promotion of our riches, our complacency and disinterest is perpetuated while we remain financially comfortable.

The problem is that to be left-wing or right-wing is in itself valueless. After the Berlin Wall crumbled, left and right came to mean so much less. And given that 'we are all now capitalists' and our approach to policy consistently so, the terms are less relevant than ever. Left and right in mainstream politics today is not, necessarily or in itself, to hold any ideological position or to denote any degree of consistency. Why for instance does the self-titled mainstream left not meaningfully defend the environment at the expense of wealth and economic growth? Perhaps the answer has something to do with philosophical thinking which is rarely described, primarily, as left or right wing. These 'descriptors' fail to describe, especially during these decades of acceptance. But they have rarely been accurate.

Even philosophy traditionally associated with the left or the right is inadequately served by these idioms. To the extent that he rejected democracy and mistrusted the abilities of the individual, requiring an absolute ruler to bind peoples to one another, Thomas Hobbes could be said to be right-wing. Marxist revolution, on the other hand, would replace democracy with subjugation of the individual for the benefit of the majority, can be described as left-wing. Without exploring the subtleties of these very different beliefs, their tenants have distinct parallels. Even in context the definitions are problematic. If these two philosophies were to be taken as 'bookends' of left and right, it cannot be said that a philosophy which, say, champions the individual over society is either right or left wing. John Locke set out what we understand by liberal democracy today, constitutional government with the consent of the people. Locke proffered that men are born equal; in 'the state of nature' men are free, enjoying natural 'God given' rights. Similarly, J. S. Mill argued government's obligation was to remove the barriers to individual behaviour that are of no harm to others.[12] Does this not make them a diametric opposite of not only Hobbes, but also Karl Marx?[13] And if so, how does the left-right spectrum help to characterise these most considered of political beliefs?

There is of course the political spectrum examined as circular, rather than the linear extremes, that places extreme left and extreme right close together, fascism being far nearer to communism than conservatism; communism closer to fascism than democratic socialism. Mainstream conservatism and social democracy (or democratic socialism to raise that old debate) have something in common that is a world away from their excessive brethren, something that unites 'centre ground' politics and that is the powerful ideal of democracy. But an adherence to democracy and more centre ground politics only serves to re-introduce the linear nature of left and right and to highlight the truth that to be a democrat is not to be left or right wing. In our own times they perpetuate a fiction of political change and feed a discourse while allowing a two decade long narrowing of our economic destiny.

While left-right can and should be criticised, such terms are not, however, wholly redundant and to describe politics without its simple and, yes, effective label becomes harder and less immediate. The expressions are also, probably here to stay, having, after all, survived since the eighteenth century. Left and right as terms are, nevertheless, insufficient and must not be allowed to prevent progression in the second decade. A number of political scientists have, over the years, critiqued the left–right axis. Many have questioned the polar extremes of communism–fascism and have proposed alternatives including pacifism–militarism; democracy–oligarchy; radicalism–conservatism; conflict resolution of conversation–negotiation–force;[14] interventionism–isolationism. Others have proposed multi-axis models, notably the psychologist Hans Eysenck whose 1961 model added a vertical authoritarian–democratic axis[15] and David Nolan's 'Nolan Chart' which includes the degree of economic and personal freedom permitted demonstrating that libertarianism is not exclusively left or right.[16] These revisions demonstrate that in themselves left–right takes no account of the political environment or circumstance, the degree of progression or libertarian intent (or otherwise) or even, despite its usefulness distinguishing centre ground from extremes, how democratic the subject is. Moreover, we rarely employ these models to understand the collusion between voters and politicians.

Further, issues of importance to a polity might not accurately be described as falling into these neat categories. And individual politicians or political programmes can be difficult to categorise, combining traditional left and right wing themes. And while parties are closer than ever, if we are ever to tackle the wicked problems it is essential that politics becomes more honest, more fluid and more prepared to be brave within the spectrum.

Whatever model one employs, the traditional application is often to compare competing programmes. But where such analysis can tease out the nuances of party positions, far more interesting is to observe the general trend within and between Western democracies over the period in which the mixed economic settlement became entrenched. Here the thrust of politics centred on our riches can be mapped. For the nuances are incremental, whereas the thrust includes the big changes, consolidation and ultimately consensus.

Nuances, Sophistication and Progression

To determine a position on the political spectrum depends on the ability to either categorise an assortment of beliefs in some consistently wrapped position, or that one or two dominant beliefs define ones position over all others. This is nearly always how politics is characterised. And yet sophisticated politics should require politicians and parties to hold views across a range of subjects with the broad political, economic, social and global environment providing severe limitations on any practical position. It is not to be inconsistent to think through each position independently, to hold views in one policy area caricatured as left and in another area as right. It is consistent if for no other reason than the left-right spectrum is flawed. Furthermore, some policy areas, such as the environment, which may have in the past been dropped with insufficient thought on the left, fail to be so easily the preserve of one or other wing.

It is not only capitalists whose interests lie in industrial growth, it is workers too whose jobs depend upon it. And it is most likely the wealthier property owners who object to the countryside being built on to provide housing for those in need. Eco-warriors campaigning against road building may consider themselves as lefties, but blue rinse middle class ladies like to preserve their green and pleasant country villages just as much.

153

Nevertheless, such examples represent interest rather than principle; 'bread and butter' politics as it were. And this is a distinction that must be drawn. Our politics, over two decades at least, has only come to constrain our willingness to pursue policy for its broader ideological principle than for maximising our bread and butter. Our riches now define political discourse making it increasingly less relevant.

In any case, just what does it mean to be on the left or the right? Laissez-faire and promoting traditional values have come to be associated with the right. Interventionism and lifestyle tolerance is proudly owned by the left. Few stop to consider that such positions, viewed in these terms, are contradictory. Laissez-faire by definition is to promote freedom of individual action; planning and intervention, interferes with individuals' lives. This is not to argue that there is little difference between these competing positions. Most obviously the acceptance or rejection of inequality, distinguishes these stances. What it does argue, nevertheless, is that a simple left-right axis does not explain why if a politician is collectivist he or she should endorse individual expression or if another politician is laissez-faire he or she should be interested in private life conformity. It is, however, a nod to the mixed economic settlement where conflicting forms of liberalism have been embraced by mainstream politics.

The last remaining ideological divisions in democratic, Western, government appear to be subtle differences about the role of the state and its connotations for authority, authoritarianism and control of liberties combined with a division of attitude between conservatism and progressive approaches which is not reflective of the linear political spectrum. But such nuances tend to be at the margins given the conformity of contemporary politics, seen in the differences between the European social model compared to the American business model (and even within Europe when one compares the equality outcomes of state policy in places like Denmark with the likes of the UK).

To be arrested for reading out names of war dead, for shouting 'rubbish' at a government minister, for wearing slogans decrying a country's foreign policy; removing the right to religious expression; imprisonment for a thought or holding an unpalatable view; suppression of a relatively mainstream academic book. These are all acts of state or societal control against the minority or the individual. And these acts are not just to be associated with un-democratic, repressive regimes. Each of these examples have taken place in Europe or the United States during the first decade of the twenty first century while we were accepting and cementing the mixed economic settlement.[17] It is easy to characterise such control as a right wing process, but the suppression of ideas in Europe is most likely to be the suppression of 'right-wing' ideas, when judged by its own terms.

The subjugation of the individual over society is as likely to be associated with the collectivist left than the capitalist right, to again judge by these terms. So is individual freedom or a belief in self-expression a right or left wing issue? The answer is neither. What is being described is not the imposition of right or left-wing politics in the containment of individualism, but rather slinking authoritarianism of state or society over that which it does not approve or finds a threat. And the dissent is seen as a threat to our riches or indeed to the capacity of the state to protect them. It is part of the narrowing of our economic destiny. Authoritarianism, especially when considered within democratic society, does not fit neatly into left or right descriptors. To an extent these bear little relationship with our riches beyond falling outside of conformity of policy directed towards promotion of our financial interests and shared across the West.

Returning to the question of Locke and Mill posed a paragraph or three ago, their awkwardness of categorisation in left – right terms emanates from their anti-authoritarianism, their libertarian, liberal or progressive nature. After all, John Stuart Mill (born 1806) believed in female suffrage denied to British women until 1918,[18] the abolition of slavery which did not occur in American until 1865[19] as well as the sort of progressive electoral system which, even in the twenty-first century is yet to be enjoyed by Britons or Americans. And yet few serious politicians would today advocate the regressive step of removing votes from women, or re-introducing slavery (or even a return to the segregation endured in some southern US states until as recently as the mid 1960s). And the reason they would not advocate this retreat is because they have accepted the political progression. It is about understanding how policy is formed. Here we return to the ideas of incrementalism in policy, building on that which went before it albeit with 'punctuated equilibrium'.

Two-hundred years ago, to advocate female suffrage would have been considered as radical. Not, of course, today. To this extent political views must be contextualised but also probed for their own worth. To be progressive in itself, is not to be left, right or centre. But to be progressive, as described here, is to hold values absent from simple left or right. That 'progression' in terms of the mixed economic settlement has come to cement these three strands of policy firmly into place.

Indeed what now represents the mainstream 'left' has rather given up on the idea of freedom; dismissing it as some sort of libertarian 'right wing' agenda. Progressively, these strands developed and in the decades of acceptance means that regression is unlikely to happen in any serious way, building on incremental change. But in narrowing our ambitions, it has also constrained what policy can do for our wellbeing.

And yet with policy directed toward wealth creation and protecting global capitalism, such issues are not priorities and neither is completing the mixed economic settlement project. It is indeed a tragedy of our riches. Politicians have to conform to be elected; they have to be categorised because the system punishes disunity. In this respect it is ironic that we criticise 'on message politicians' but eject from office parties which appear divided. If the next stage is to be political reform then our polity is stubbornly unsupportive. The conformity is about who can best protect our wealth which is why we have an intolerant debate over issues such as prisons and immigration where the popularist is the enemy of the sensible.

A rather striking example here is that argument over crime and punishment with successive governments accepting British Home Secretary Michael Howard's 1990s mantra that 'prison works' in the face of almost all academic research to the contrary. Over the twenty years since 1990, and under Conservative and Labour administrations, the British prison population doubled to over 90,000 inmates (mostly men) and yet the statistics showed that for shorter sentences such action encouraged re-offending. Alas, it was easier to make the emotive 'lock 'em up' argument than the more sophisticated case to tackle causes and rehabilitation. Indeed, there are more votes in the former and the system forced political programmes to comply.

During the good economic times, it also served public policy since it tackled rather swiftly those who threatened society directed towards the promotion of our riches. Extraordinarily, it was only after the 2010 general election when the priority for short term economic policy was to cut spending, that the case was made by Conservative Lord Chancellor Ken Clarke to reduce the cost of prisons by reducing the number of inmates and simultaneously being more considered about tackling offenders. It was not popular with the red-top press. And after the 2011 riots became once again politically difficult.

This is perhaps why the genuine idea of left and right, in mainstream domestic, democratic politics and in wider international relations has become harder to maintain. This is part of the mixed economic settlement. There was a time, not so very long ago, when the dividing lines of politics were clearer cut. The cold-war which divided the world between the democratic West and the communist East; the realities of post-war Europe which meant welfarism and even through consensus ones attitudes to the changes could be caricatured; the political climate in Europe which led to the riots of 1968 pitched elements of society against the state; Thatcherism in Britain and Reaganomics in the US, redefined mainstream politics and eventually defeated a prominent 'left'. But in doing this they preserved some elements of welfare liberalism. No longer can such dividing lines be so elegantly drawn in political life and yet the outdated and increasingly irrelevant left-right divide is obstinately clung to.

Stephen Barber

Political Tribes and the Democracy we have Bought

Left and right survive as terms because they ease the description of politicians, parties, governments and policies. It is simpler to describe a political view as left wing or right wing or even centre ground than it is to properly communicate its values and ideological core. Here, journalists, politicians and even academics are perhaps sometimes wantonly languid and inaccurate in their analysis.

There is another reason, however, which cannot be lain quite so readily at the feet of political scientists or commentators and it is key to understanding why the unsustainable cheat has survived. Tribalism is a bewildering force in (party) politics. It can obscure and stifle as much as re-enforce values. It exists because of the powerful system of party politics entrenched in most modern democracies and which are the great structural issues in tackling the tragedy of our riches. Members of one party can far easier discern a political enemy by the colour of their rosette than by a comparison of the views and values they hold. Indeed, tribalism can even negate the need for consistently held values since the identifier of belonging to a party (often with a choice of two or three serious national political parties in a given polity) and the commonly held conception of where that party sits between left and right is enough to define someone's politics.

The British economist James Rockey went so far as to analyse this and discovered that as we get older we are more likely to misplace ourselves in the political spectrum, identifying ourselves as far more 'left wing' and consequently with parties 'of the left' than our views would objectively justify. 'The broad conclusion of the paper must be that individuals either choose not to, or are unable to, locate their ideological positions reliably compared to those of the positions of their compatriots... this is further evidence not just that voters are far from fully informed, but that somehow voters consistently mis-perceive where they lie on the ideological spectrum'.[20] This is all an unfortunate reflection on political discourse since it forces people of differing opinion in one party to maintain the fiction of solidarity while simultaneously masking genuine agreement with members of a separate party sometimes with boorishness and aggression. It also allows democratic discourse to continue irrespective of the mixed economic settlement which most democratic politicians seem to buy into. Here, the political tribes take their positions – positions of rhetoric rather than ideology – and exaggerate the differences reflective of consumer society. The tribes, substantially, take the place of political thought.

The tribes engage in a dishonesty which sustains or at least allows them to dominate a democracy and perpetuates the cheat. Indeed the 'conspiracy' among parties is to pitch a battle of tribes rather than a battle of ideas. Really difficult decisions are rarely debated and certainly not in any detailed sense and certainly not during election campaigns. Plato's 'noble lie' (found in *The Republic*) advocates lying for moral ends. The moral ends in modern democracy is the need to take the 'right' decisions, which our political leaders very often do and honourably so. The lie, noble or otherwise, is the dilution of debate to sound bites and superficially petty point scoring. Indeed, as Peter Oborne observes, Western democracies 'have tended to adopt a model of addressing the electorate very similar to and to a very large extent drawn from advertising copy: brief, simplistic and often deceitful.'[21] Disraeli's 'greasy pole' that politicians must climb which represents compromise after compromise begins at candidate selection and becomes more pronounced in the campaign and beyond. Some would say it is about balancing interests. But the compromise means those at the top, in all tribes, reaching a consistent consensus. It also means that contradictory, wicked, demands of electors must be humoured and any threat to our riches avoided. Is it any wonder that as we eschew competing ideologies, our economic destiny has been constricted?

Michael Bloomberg

According to Forbes Magazine, New York Mayor and founder of the financial media giant which bears his name, is worth some $20 billion putting Michael Bloomberg in the top ten richest Americans.[22] Who can say whether it is the power that accompanies such great wealth or the kind of driven personality which it takes to acquire it, that has allowed Bloomberg to flout the usual conventions of tribal politics? Harbouring ambitions to succeed Mayor Giuliani, this lifelong Democrat jettisoned his party in 2001 to join the Republicans, contest and win the race against a number of long-established figures. There was a view that the Democrats would take the election and Bloomberg switched parties with the pragmatic logic that securing the Democratic nomination would be more difficult given the crowded field. Running against Herman Badillo, he snatched the Republican nomination by a margin of 2:1.

The Democratic primary had been expensive for winner Mark Green and in the subsequent election, taking place in the shadow of the September 11 terrorist attacks, was massively outspent by Bloomberg who narrowly beat him at the polls. Having won re-election by a much wider margin in 2005, Bloomberg decided to quit the Republicans in 2007, issuing a statement which read:

> *I have filed papers with the New York City Board of Elections to change my status as a voter and register as unaffiliated with any political party. Although my plans for the future haven't changed, I believe this brings my affiliation into alignment with how I have led and will continue to lead our city.*
>
> *A nonpartisan approach has worked wonders in New York: we've balanced budgets, grown our economy, improved public health, reformed the school system and made the nation's safest city even safer.*[23]

While this fuelled speculation that New York might be a mere stepping stone for Bloomberg's ambitions, the day before he had spoken at 'Ceasefire: bridging the political divide conference' where he had told delegates:

> *We do not have to settle for the same old politics. We do not have to accept the tired debate between the left and right, between Democrats and Republicans, between Congress and the White House. We can and we must declare a ceasefire - and move America forward.*

> *While a ceasefire is essential, it must also be followed*
> *by change. Real change - not the word, but the deed.*
> *Not slogans, but a fundamentally different way of*
> *behaving - one built on cooperation and collaboration.*
> *And it is needed now - because more than ever,*
> *Washington is sinking into a swamp of dysfunction. No*
> *matter who's in charge, sadly today, Partisanship is*
> *King.[24]*

Cynics dismiss Bloomberg as an opportunist who uses the party system to achieve his personal ambitions irrespective of the values they embody. Having made his great fortune, he wanted great power and the White House represented the summit of these ambitions. But one might also ask why someone like Bloomberg, or indeed any of us, should be forced to categorise their politics in the rigid confines of one machine or another, particularly given the demise of traditional divisions. After all, while Bloomberg can be accused of using the party system to his own advantage, it is difficult to argue that he is without thought through ideas, or that he reads from the script of a pre-prepared, focus group guided, party manifesto. His politics are a cross spectrum mix of economic conservatism and social liberalism. One could argue that to hold thought through positions as opposed to the tribalism of convention is only a credit to him.

Political Malaise

One consequence of the decline in politics, tribalism and our comfortable, rich, lives is the limited interest most people have in politics. In developed Western democracies, there is a palpable malaise in voter sentiment if not towards politics generally then certainly in respect of political parties. Turnout has generally declined and membership of political parties has gradually dissipated. This is explained in part by our rather natural inclination towards complacency during times of economic prosperity.

It is the self-serving economic 'culture of contentment' that Galbraith described when he made the case that 'in the future, near or far, a candidate for the American presidency will emerge who is committed to the human needs and remedies... And perhaps, if the electorate is enlarged to include the economically and socially now-disenfranchised, he or she will succeed and bring along a favouring majority in the Congress. As I said before, the prospect is not bright.'[25] But more than that, there are macro-social developments, some of which have been discussed in this chapter, which have served to constrain not only policy makers but also faith in politics. Paul Webb makes the point:

> *These factors help us understand why parties (particularly since the end of the long post-war boom) have suffered from the widespread perception of policy ineffectiveness; the apparent failures of government to resolve persistent national policy problems are bound to undermine the popular status of parties – especially when these failures are associated with more than one party in a system.*[26]

Citing Budge and Kemen,[27] he goes on to argue that party influenced government is still able to create positive policy outputs. In democratic discourse, however, tribal competition serves only to widen the divide between parties themselves and the party political system with voters.

There are two developments or at least examples of our politics, which demonstrate progression in bridging that divide. The Tea Party movement in the United States and coalition government of quite different parties in the United Kingdom are a challenge to simple tribalism. As this chapter will argue, they are insufficient in their reach but in their respective endeavours could teach the other an important lesson about the need to improve political discourse.

The Tea Party

The Tea Party is an unusual beast; grassroots and 'traditionally American', it has been unafraid to express some hard line views which are not always widely popular.[28] But regardless of one's sympathies with its sentiments – small government, limited taxation and public spending, libertarianism and adherence to the constitution - it can be seen as an encouraging re-engagement of people into the political process. The movement is just that. It is neither a political party nor a formally organised political body. It has not sought election nor does it have a national leader. Furthermore, and rather crucially, it is not a single issue pressure group as we have come to recognise, but rather is an umbrella for an ideologically consistent approach. Taking its name from the Boston Tea Party where in 1773 colonists revolted against their British rulers, the modern incarnation emerged in 2009 and really took hold (as 'a sleeping giant awakened') during the often hostile debates over President Obama's healthcare reform plans. One thing this reminds politicians is that while we tend to think of class conflict as the poor revolting against the rich, a problem for policymakers is that of exit. It started to happen in the 1980s and is a problem when the 'rich' resist paying for services they do not use and do not want.

Democrats have more often been at the sharp end of the Tea Party's ire with one Democratic commentator, Kristin Sosaine, telling Fox News that the two are indistinguishable, 'the Republican Tea Party', as she described it.[29] But this is not, entirely, fair. Republican figures have been strongly associated with the Tea Party and that association has increased the likelihood of election. And there are big names like Rand Paul and Sarah Palin which the movement counts among its most prominent supporters. Indeed, it has supported a number of populist challengers to more mainstream politicians as John McCain himself found when he had to fight off a primary bid for his 2010 Arizona Senate nomination by a right wing radio host. A consequence of this association or even reliance is a palpable shift in the centre of Republican gravity to this rightward, libertarian position, lest they see a split of the vote as the Democrats once did with the experience of Ralph Nader's Presidential candidacy. It resulted in a rather 'oddball field of Republican candidates'[30] for the 2010 midterms.

But the crucial feature here is that the Tea Party is not a coherent political force trying to win elections. It is a community, locally and nationally based movement, which wants its voice heard by candidates and elected politicians. In this respect it has been successful in its short existence. As the 'Tea Partier' Doug Mainwaring put it in the Washington Post, 'The movement has nothing to do with Democrat versus Republican politics and power. It has everything to do with the

American people versus the hubris of politics as usual in Washington. The existence of the Tea Party movement is Main Street America's indictment against the ruling class.'[31]

While a welcome re-engagement of people in their communities and in their politics, the dangers of the Tea Party are its narrow viewpoint and tendency towards the extreme right with at least an undercurrent of racism. Rand Paul, for instance questioned the constitutional relevance for business of the Civil Rights Act.[32] While later distancing himself from the idea, the Tea Party is still perhaps providing an opportunity and a pressure for mainstream party elites to move further away from consensus.

Cameron, Clegg and the Lib-Con Experiment in 'New Politics'

The Liberal Democrat elder statesman Sir Menzies Campbell made a throwaway remark during a broadcast interview: 'If you have a dog for long enough you come to look like your pet,' he told the presenter Andrew Neil, 'people with coalition partners come to look like their coalition partners'.[33] Throwaway it might have been, but it was such a cutting line that Ming repeated it on a much more mainstream BBC documentary on the new government.

Britain's first coalition government since the Second World War, a 'delicate monster' if ever there were, was forged by a growing trust and respect of two men: Conservative leader David Cameron and Liberal Democrat leader Nick Clegg. Unlike many of their party colleagues, these two men seemed to slip into the habit of working together with consummate ease. And they did look ever more alike, their physical resemblance and personal chemistry, 'the brokeback coalition' as it was mocked, ever more obvious. Of the coalition negotiations, 'we surprised each other', said Clegg. 'It felt like things were beginning to click into place,' said Cameron.[34] For Margaret Thatcher, a very different Tory leader, compromise was a dirty word which prevented difficult decisions from being taken. But in its early days the coalition found itself confidently making bold, brave and unpopular policy.

An unusual paring in many ways, it was a 'generational thing' according to Campbell who, like many in his party, had always wanted a realignment of the 'left' in Grimond's tradition. It might, too, have represented the path of least resistance or as newly elected Labour MP and a next generation politician, Emma Reynolds put it 'the coalition agreement is a lowest common denominator document'. Or even the idea that 'there was a desire but no necessity to form a coalition in 1997. In 2010, there was a necessity but no desire.'[35] But it also demonstrated the difficulties of categorising left and right without also considering authoritarianism versus libertarianism as well as the potential strengths of two political traditions combining for a common purpose.

Partially the 'new politics' heralded in the aftermath of agreement was simply a novelty because the British political system, indeed even the construction of the Commons chamber, requires adversarial politics. There are two lines of opposing benches with lines drawn down each side, two sword widths apart, that members bust stand behind when speaking. The Chamber was destroyed during a bombing raid in the Second World War. Churchill had the option of rebuilding in a consensual, semi-circular format, but instead ordered that it rebuilt exactly as it was; too small to accommodate all members. Adjust to new politics which meant co-operation, compromise, consensus and discussion, was not a natural process.

And it is here that there was the starkest contrast between the party squabbles of the campaign and the maturity of coalition politics. The great and novel feature of the 2010 election campaign was the leaders' debates. The experience as a whole was a dramatic turnaround from party leaders finding differences in their policies to constructive coalition discussions between Lib Dem and Conservative teams after the election where the process was about finding common ground and agreement between programmes. That represented, however brief, a healthy addition to what has become rather unsatisfactory and tribal politics in Britain. But its maintenance of political elites rather than genuine partnership beyond party meant that its ambitions in this respect would always be limited.

Politics Becomes Difficult

Making one of his rare forays into the political arena, former British prime minister John Major gave evidence to the respected House of Commons Public Administration Select Committee where he made the argument that politics has become more difficult since the 'easy things have been done, the difficult things remain to be done.'[36] Given the great ideological struggles and the political strain from which the mixed economic settlement emerged, this might be considered to be a rather perplexing statement. After all, if the big arguments have been fought and peace treaties signed, one might expect politics to be easier, more pragmatic. But in a post-ideological environment it becomes more difficult to take difficult or at least unpopular decisions since the electorate itself is less tribal and less divided and because of the wicked problems discussed earlier. Thus, where explicit consensus is absent from tribal party politics, there is a disincentive for government to take right but unpopular decisions. As Emily Dickenson put it, 'the soul selects her own society; then shuts the door on her divine majority.'

There is, nonetheless, evidence of new emerging themes where more subtle yet different ideological positions are surfacing. In the aftermath of the credit crunch there is more confidence than there has been in decades in the formal idea of the state, its role and power over our lives (albeit undermined by the reassertion of the markets). There is an opposing trend, emerging from, but not confined to, free market conservatism, not simply in the Reaganite more minimal state but more substantially in self-determining societies which can exercise power at a local level. What is notable is that while the power of the market is acknowledged and still to some degree embraced, there is a confidence in complementary ideas. In what otherwise began as a rather cynical display of party politics, before the innovative leaders' debate proved transformative, these ideas appeared to emerge during the 2010 British general election campaign and subsequent coalition government. They are played out in the United States. And it can be seen reflected in the practical politics of reducing public spending in Europe and across other parts of the world. Indeed, these ideas are contextualised by the new globalised world.

The wicked problems discussed in this chapter highlight three things. Firstly, that some policies contradict, creating tensions in our demands and in and between our societies; secondly, that in a post ideological polity not only are the 'right' answers not located exclusively with one side of the political spectrum but they are no longer ideologically grounded; and thirdly society has to accept that everyone cannot be satisfied all of the time. Post ideological politics also requires a more consensual system if it is to begin to adequately tackle these big and emerging issues. Quite unlike the ideological governments of the past when majoritarianism (or something which resembled it) was sufficient mandate for great policy change given the dogmatic belief that it was right, pragmatic and constrained policymaking of today needs to embrace. The fact that the 2010 British coalition government is the first in more than sixty five years to command more than fifty percent of votes cast at the election has not prevented the opposition from questioning its legitimacy in a way that was never made of the ideologically driven Thatcher governments of the 1980s which enjoyed little more than forty percent of the vote (although healthy majorities in Parliament). But it is the coalition which is closer to how politics needs to be; comprised of politicians from parties of different traditions in this case the Conservatives and Liberal Democrats. Incidentally, there are reasons to see these two old political traditions as complementary despite the tensions between them. They have worked together before (through the Second World War, the national government of 1931, and during the great Lloyd George coalition), there is a libertarian and open market streak running through each and the Conservative party is perhaps the most adaptable of political parties in modern history.

Simple majority supported policy is much less sustainable now than it once was. Policy needs to be widely supported while accepting that everyone cannot be satisfied absolutely all of the time. And values should not be absent, to be replaced by a passionless, managerial, bureaucratic pragmatism. Combined visions can be far more powerful, displacing the lazy idea of diluted compromise. One member of that coalition government, the Conservative David Willetts, for instance described how the political tension between the partners was positive:

> *We come from different backgrounds and different parties. However, we work together day in, day out and I actually think it improves the quality of decision taking. What you find is that you have to offer evidence; you are challenged and questioned by someone from a different political party... It leads to better, more open, more transparent decision taking and working together is what the British people expect us to do.*[37]

Such coalitions are commonplace across Europe and to varying degrees of success. Belgium's rather comical nine and a half months of negotiations to deliver a government compares poorly with the stable and strong coalitions formed in Germany. Indeed, in 2005 a second grand coalition of the CDU and SPD lasted until 2009, providing stability and leadership throughout the credit crunch. And the presidential system of the United States requires the commander in chief to form alliances with other parties in Congress and during less ideological times in the make up of Cabinet. It sometimes works.

But this has to extend further than co-operation between parties and draw in civil society itself. It is insufficient simply for the citizens to 'expect' certain behaviour from those in power and instead needs to form partnerships in the creation and implementation of political agendas. Policy cannot simply be owned by a party or even a combination of parties. And it is here that the Tea Party movement provides something of an inspiration irrespective of one's opinions of its members' views. The movement is comprised differing yet intellectually coherent ideas about the way America should be governed. And it is truly a grassroots association, springing up in communities across the United States. Where it is left wanting, however, is in its connections with organised politics. While it has wedged itself into the Republican Party, it has done so parochially, pressurising candidates into supporting a very narrow, and sometimes extreme, view of policy.

'New politics' in the United Kingdom has made progress in building consensus across the political spectrum but in doing so at the elite level of party politics, it needs to find grassroots partners. What it was able to achieve in a political sense, however, has been limited as its political capital was rapidly spent. Politics cannot be simply something which state elites 'do to voters' for their own good. Likewise, a conservative movement like the Tea Party would benefit from forging much broader links with elite politics and perhaps it needs to find a liberal coalition partner at the top of electoral politics nationally and in the States. It is in this way that politics can claim post-majoritarian legitimacy. There must be greater collectivity, less tribalism and a will to tackle the difficult issues that have so far been cheated.

Why the State is not the Answer

Democratic political rhetoric so often talks about the need to 'engage with voters'. And what is equally true is that, save for an activist and interested minority, politics is all too usually a turn off for most people. Political elites engaging in dialogues with those they serve is to be welcomed but it cannot be a solution itself. Political elites alone cannot own politics and policy. And while we cling obstinately to the notion that the state is the singular solution to our problems, the unsustainable cheat will be perpetuated. Policy must be owned outside of the state and state institutions for post-majoritarian politics to prosper.

The more sophisticated debate Margaret Thatcher sought to enter about the existence of society, is germane to the discussion since while she was wrong - there is such thing as society - simply more of the state only serves to make us more individualistic. The state is not the alternative to the individual. That is not to say that the welfare liberalism of Attlee, which became the first strand of the mixed economic settlement, eroded society; it did not and indeed in reducing inequalities made for more cohesive wellbeing. But that cannot produce a logic whereby more state equals increasingly better societies. Responsibility, individual and societal, is itself increasingly absent where a centralised state controls and standardises; especially so where its vision is so narrowly focussed upon the creation of riches. There is no need for morality or indeed incentive for individual or community engagement where the tentacles of the state direct policy from the centre.

Like other areas of thought (not least free markets), Margaret Thatcher succeeded in contaminating the brand of the direction of this argument. One can see such in the ideas of Friedrich Hayek, long associated with Thatcherism, but who nonetheless stood as a liberal figure with a hopeful vision of human nature. In *The Constitution of Liberty* he made the powerful argument that it is 'because we do not know how individuals will use their freedom that it is so important. If it were otherwise, the results of freedom could also be achieved by the majority's deciding what should be done by the individuals.'[38] And so not only is individual freedom important but so is individual responsibility within family, community, society and even internationally.

The state has long been accused of economic crowding out – that is it provides services which the private or indeed voluntary sector might otherwise be expected to offer or causing a reduction in private demand resulting from increased taxation. But we might also suffer from its crowding out of citizens' ownership of politics. It is a point made by Mark Littlewood who makes the case that 'the more the government is providing to your neighbours, friends, work colleagues and relatives, the less obliged you feel to act yourself.'[39] While there is democratic accountability, this chapter has discussed the limitations inherent in existing systems, especially as politics has become post-ideological. Hayek himself made the point during criticisms of the Lib Lab pact in the late 1970s. In a letter to the London *Times* he warned about unlimited democracy in which, 'government loses the power even to do what it thinks right if any group on which its majority depends thinks otherwise.'[40] While Hayek was defending the alternate idea of individual near *market democracy*, something which had yet to find its place in the mixed economic settlement, there is a truism about short-term party politics which is not always good for political decision making. This has only become more acute as politics becomes more difficult. In building post-majoritarian politics, the state will need to be checked in terms of its pervading, centralised, reach into society.

So the state has its part to play in dealing with politics as it becomes more difficult. But it can never be the solution alone. Democratic politics is to be cherished but the power which has been assumed by party tribes and political elites has prevented a broadening of our economic vision.

The Big Society

David Cameron's 'big idea' was called 'the big society'. And while both he and his party struggled to define the concept (even being reported as an electoral hindrance by Conservative candidates in the 2010 general election), it was both something of a response to the challenge described here and an idea to which Cameron was committed. Cameron adviser Ian Birrell tried to clarify by describing it as 'an attempt to connect the civic institutions that lie between the individual and the state... In political terms, this means passing power to the lowest level possible: radical public service reform... To amplify the devolution of power there must be greater transparency, freeing up the state's information and data.'[41] And in the most thoughtful exposition of the big society, politician and thinker Jesse Norman went so far as to argue that, 'we have reached the limits of the idea of the state as a remedy for social and economic failure. What is so striking is how impoverished political debate has become on these issues, and how reliant we are on a single and inflexible model of state provision of public services to solve our social ills.[42] Such a fuzzy concept could have profound implications.

But how does such a big society fit into the mixed economic settlement? The answer, in part, lies in the mid 1990s when Tony Blair as *New* Labour leader adopted the idea of the 'stakeholder society'. There are clear parallels between the two concepts and in each case it was about distancing from the popular political legacy of Thatcher while wholeheartedly embracing Thatcherism economically.[43] The common positive use of 'society' immediately contrasts with Thatcher's famous (and often misquoted) interview with Woman's Own magazine in 1987: '...they are casting their problems on society and who is society? There is no such thing! There are individual men and women and there are families and no government can do anything except through people and people look to themselves first.'[44] The phrase that became associated with her was 'there's no such thing as society' and it painted the Thatcherite Conservatives as simply uncaring. Also the 1980s was a divisive decade where individualism split society and split domestic politics. But as this book has argued, neo-liberal, market led economic policy has become a fundamental part of the mixed economic settlement.

For Blair in the 1990s and more recently for Cameron, their respective stakeholder and big societies enabled them to distance themselves from the 'uncaring' image of Thatcherism with the language of inclusiveness. After all, it suited Blair to adopt (briefly) the Conservative idea of 'one nationism' because at the time the Tories were hopelessly split and he was promoting a 'big tent' approach to politics. For Cameron, coalition and the need for harsh spending cuts meant the phrase 'we are all in this together' tripped easily off ministers' tongues. But in doing this, each was able to embrace wholeheartedly the economic settlement bequeathed by Thatcher.

The stakeholder society failed to gain traction with the public and Blair ruthlessly dropped the idea before its 1997 electoral test; rarely to be heard of again. The big society survived in part because of the personal commitment of Prime Minister Cameron and in part because of its practical application. While thinkers behind the big society, such as Norman, might have wanted, 'a philosophy: a concerted and wide-ranging attempt to engage with the twin challenges of social and economic decline, and move towards a more connected society',[45] the realpoliticks of the time saw it as more consequential. Despite the believers' best attempts, the danger for the big society was that emerging parallel to the higher priority deep cuts in public spending, rather than confronting the challenge outlines by this book, it became a proxy for financially squeezed public services. When thousands of protestors descended on London in March 2011 to protest at public spending cuts, opposition leader Ed Miliband was able to declare before the assembled crowd, 'David Cameron, this is the big society'. In a sense he was right and the government's vulnerability for promoting the big society but not using it to form permanent political partnerships into communities was laid bare.

Confronting the Challenge

As politics becomes more difficult there is and will be the clear option to concede or to confront and doing the former is simply unsustainable. There is a wonderful exchange between the academic and writer Tony Judt and his 14 year old son Daniel, published in the *New York Times*. In response to Daniel's disappointment at President Obama's willingness to face up to the big issues notably the environment ('I have become hugely pessimistic about the moral resolve of our government and corporate world'), Tony writes:

> *I did vote for Barack Obama. I held out no great hopes. It was clear from the outset that this was someone who would concede rather than confront — and that's a shortcoming in a politician, if not in a man.... Actually, while I agree that we need to build a national consensus, I don't think the challenge is to convince Americans about pollution or even climate change. Nor is it just a matter of getting them to make sacrifices for the future. The challenge is to convince them once again of how much they could do if they came together.... it is not beyond us to sacrifice in the present for long-term advantage, to set aside the pursuit of quarterly economic growth as the supreme goal of public policy. We offer ourselves easy choices — high taxation or free markets — and are then surprised to learn that they do not speak to our needs.*[46]

This cheat really is unsustainable and in a post-ideological environment, politicians must draw a line under their

179

willingness to agree to conflicting policy. Looking across our politics today and there is a stranglehold of professional actors no longer interested in taking the most difficult of decisions or contributing to the development of a destiny. Political tribes protect our riches while the old left right mainstream, long ago fading into meaninglessness, provides a useful cover for those wanting to be identified with political tradition. But the system punishes honesty and those offering stark, unpopular, and even unavoidable choices. It is a problem for both politicians and society. And so too must electors accept that there are real and necessary choices which mean we cannot always have it all and have it now. The prize in creating a new, political, strand to the settlement can be a fresh destiny.

Before this can happen, though, there either needs to be a new puncture in the equilibrium with an emerging ideological divide, or at least some breakdown in the hold of the party political tribes. Moving beyond majoritarianism, not only in administrative formation but also in policy terms is the first step and the new politics (promised fleetingly by the UK coalition) is a healthy example of this. But politics cannot be something which is 'done to' ordinary people. Politics and policy cannot simply reside with state elites who 'know better'. New partnerships must be formed with conventional politics and these must grow from society upwards, not as lobby or pressure groups, but as ideologically consistent community enterprises.

Chapter Seven

Our Age of Anxiety

One might diagnose something of a collective psychosis at work in our rich societies. We are wealthy, consumer driven, gleefully wasteful but also communally insecure. Decades of wealth creation and trickledown Reaganomics have left us with comfortable and yet disparate lifestyles. We are richer, our economic needs are ostensibly fulfilled, and yet we appear to be unhappy and demand cumulatively more of those very riches which have served our malaise. This is the consequence of narrowing the vision of our economic destiny which was exacerbated under the reign of the baby boomers during the two decades of mixed economic acceptance.

Robert Frank's account of 'Luxury Fever' has made this powerful case that Americans have demanded increasingly luxurious consumer goods over recent decades in the quest for happiness and following trends established by the super rich. The consequence, he argues, is not that we have become happier but that we work harder and longer to afford bigger cars and bigger houses, all at the expense of the sort of activities which genuinely make us happy, such as spending time with our families. He points out that: 'although it is the mansions of the super rich that make the news, the far more newsworthy fact is that the average house built in the United States today is nearly twice as large as its counterpart in the 1950s... No matter where you stand on the income scale, no matter how little you feel influenced by what others do, you cannot have escaped the effects of recent changes in the spending environment.'[1] Meanwhile, the world has become a more hesitant place in which we are less sure of our position, our allies and our enemies. The new uncertainties have not only left us fearful but, unlike previous adversities, they have also divided us. No more the collective fear of cold war annihilation or Blitz spirit defiance. Today we fear individually; we fear those around us. We fear the threats to our riches. Here it is the mixed economic settlement which told us that our ideas were right and with the experience of such collective fait accompli made individualism possible.

Is this a failure of government or a failure of the governed? Have we fulfilled Jeremy Bentham's utilitarian ideal of 'the greatest happiness for the greatest number is the foundation of all morals and legislation', or undermined it in the pursuit of riches? Are we rich because we are unhappy? (Or indeed unhappy because we are rich?) And perhaps that idea of 'psychosis' is not as flippant as it appears or indeed was intended when first tapped out on the keyboard. Happiness is nothing if not an emotional assessment of our own and our collective wellbeing. And yet, we all but ignore such a measure in policy.

In one very real sense, that 'metaphoric psychosis' has manifested itself in veracity. Rates of depression have increased over decades. In 2007 a report produced by the World Health Organisation and Harvard Medical School showed that the United States, the world's richest country, topped a world study of bipolar, major depressive or chronic minor depressive disorders at 9.6%. Studies suggest that it is the nature of our societies which breeds depression. Notwithstanding the propensity to report mental illness,[2] individualism appears to augment anxiety. And so in community based societies, depression is less common than in self-interested ones. As a result, we are perhaps more likely to suffer from depression in the wealth and peace of today than in the aftermath of death and destruction of war in 1945; more fundamentally, the baby boomers born after 1945 who have enjoyed the best the world has to offer, are more likely to suffer depression than those born in the early part of the twentieth century who had to endure real economic depression and degradation in the 1930s.[3] The same might be said for the thousands who claimed freedom after the Berlin Wall fell in 1989. Being trapped in the communist East was not an edifying experience for the masses of East Germans who finally tore down the divisions to the freedom and choice which was to be their prize, destiny and desert. And yet surveying the jumbled collection of expensive motor cars now congesting the roads of the former East, why is it that so many remember fondly the days when everyone drove an unreliable Trabant and economic growth was not the prime focus of policy?

The Splendid 1990s

At the very moment that the first of two planes crashed into the twin towers of New York's World Trade Centre on 11 September 2001, the curtain belatedly fell on a decade which had absorbed the qualities the baby boomers had taken for

183

granted and which had not yet noticed the fears of the future. For the developed West, at least, the 1990s was a secure decade. That fear of nuclear war had lifted with the fall of the Berlin Wall; politicians were tackling ordinary recession and then boom with policies universally accepted as correct; Fukuyama's 'end of history' meant an end to global ideological battles; it coincided with a truce too in the ideological divisions in domestic politics and we were not yet fully conscious of the ramifications of man's harm to the environment. This is where it began.

It was a splendid interlude of security, which, in consolidating the mixed economic settlement, bridged the collective anxieties of cold war with the individual anxieties of the twenty first century. And in this carefree decade, where Bill Clinton's phrase 'it's the economy stupid' epitomised policy, the victors of cold war grew richer, revelled in popular culture which distanced them from the caricatured 'greed' of the 1980s and travelled the world at a discount. Fuelled by a technology bubble, stock markets reached all time highs on the eve of the new millennium; levels which even a decade and more later have not been reached again. And it was in the 'Roaring Nineties' as Joseph Stiglitz caricatures these years, that we were promised the 'new economy', based on information and technology rather than manufacturing, and grown from the new globalisation fashioned in the American business model. 'The New Economy also promised an end to the business cycle, the ups and downs of the economy that had, until now, always been part of capitalism, as new information technologies allowed businesses to control inventories.'[4] For policy makers there was the dream of the 'Goldilocks economy': not too hot, not too cold.

Politics, in retrospect, appear far more mundane with 'pragmatism' heralded as an antidote to the ideologically divisive decade which unfolded. These were the years when British prime minister John Major's big initiative was the 'cones hotline', a short lived policy allowing drivers to report unnecessary traffic cones and a 'back to basics' rallying cry which was hijacked by the right.

But while it was a remarkably secure and stable decade for most of the developed world, it failed to engender any sense of common purpose beyond maintaining and growing our riches. As such, this was a decade which consolidated our new anxieties as much as it consolidated the settlement. The economic policies which were refined during this decade survived almost entirely intact until the credit crunch of 2008. Indeed, a certain Alan Greenspan served as the most powerful of Federal Reserve Chairmen from 1987 – 2006 under Presidents Reagan, Bush, Clinton and the other Bush. When he left office, all seemed well with recession a distant memory. Greenspan, like the rest of us, was soon to learn the flip side of that policy forged in complacency. But it is Greenspan who offers a comparison with his description of the pre-1914 world which 'seemed to be moving irreversibly toward higher levels of civility and civilisation; human society seemed perfectible.'[5] This was a Western world which had put the hardship of industrialisation behind it with the prospect of wealth, living standards and political freedoms. These few years before the destruction of war presented a brief era of security which our own cherished decade perhaps emulated.

The 1990s, splendid as they were, served to elongate working hours, improve productivity, allow us to buy more and live more luxuriously but did not provide for greater contentment when the stability was disrupted by the shocking realisation that the world was more volatile than ever. And while the policies meant a subsequent period of unheard of expansion, as the overheated world economy exploded, policies were left wanting in this singular regard.

The Happy Frenchman

French President Nicolas Sarkozy caused howls of derision in 2009 when he announced that Insee, the French Statistics Agency, would incorporate measures of happiness into its accounting for economic output and suggested that other countries follow suit by including *happiness* as a variable for calculating GDP.[6] With its shorter working week, more extensive welfare provision and a relatively weak record of economic performance, France might be expected to outpace the competition in any initial, cursory comparison. But this was not the sort of throwaway comment sometimes made by politicians for easy short-term effect (even though it seemed to subsequently fade into the ether).

This was more calculated and prepared, taking place in the Sorbonne on the first anniversary of the collapse of the global investment bank Lehman Brothers; Sarkozy flanked by two Nobel Prize winning economists who the president himself commissioned. Joseph Stiglitz and Amartya Sen along with Jean Paul Fitoussi were the big hitters at the helm of the *Commission on the Measurement of Economic Performance and Social Progress*. Its report, which came amid the worst global economic downturn since the depression, argued for:

> *...a shift in emphasis from measuring economic production to measuring people's wellbeing. And measures of wellbeing should be put in the context of sustainability... emphasising wellbeing is important because there appears to be an increasing gap between the information contained in aggregate GDP data and what counts for common people's well-being.*[7.]

Among other things, the report went on to recommend that measures of wellbeing should look at income and consumption, rather than production since 'Conflating the two can lead to misleading indications about how well-off people are and entail the wrong policy decisions. Material living standards are more closely associated with measures of net national income, real household income and consumption – production can expand while income decreases or vice versa when account is taken of depreciation, income flows into and out of a country, and differences between the prices of output and the prices of consumer products.'; that the household perspective should be emphasized as it 'should also reflect in-kind services provided by government, such as subsidized health care and educational services.'[8]

The report represented a human exposition of what economic policy is meant to do. There is a simple critique of orthodox economic thinking which the field of happiness economics has attempted to redress over the course of almost forty years of development. That is, conventional policy approaches assume that wellbeing (or a Benthamite utility) is dependent upon income which is achieved by improving economic productivity which drives national economic growth. Ergo, happiness is an economy called expansion. Such conventions have been challenged by numerous happiness economists such as Carol Graham, Richard Layard, and (one of the pioneers) Richard Easterlin amongst others. Back in 1974, Easterlin argued that there was indeed a correlation between happiness and levels of income within countries but a limited relationship when compared across countries. And so, if you are fortunate enough to live in a wealthy country, you are more likely to be happy than if you are struggling by in a poor one. But crucially, beyond a certain point of wealth sufficient to meet human needs, the correlation between increasing income and increasing happiness breaks down.[9]

Having sought to measure happiness using some thirty surveys covering nineteen countries over twenty four years between 1946-70, the *Easterlin Paradox* is somewhat profound. And it is that statistic that 'in the one national time series studied, that for the United States since 1946, higher income was not accompanied by greater happiness.... In judging their happiness, people tend to compare their actual situation with a reference standard or norm, derived from their prior and ongoing social experience.'[10] And of course, the irony is that one only has the luxury of this anxiety if one is wealthy enough to make these comparisons. The type of house, car, flat screen television we own. Despite globalisation, those of us in the developed world tend not to compare our situations with those in the developing.

There are other analysts who dispute this broad assessment. Drawing on the World Database of Happiness, Veenhoven and Hagert for instance, have used the idea of *life satisfaction* over 21 countries and 38 years between 1958 and 1996 and report a very modest connection between growth in earnings and growth in income. Indeed, as with Easterlin, in their USA specific survey the quarter century strong income growth trend is far from replicated in the happiness measure and it would not appear to be proportionate.[11] What is more striking is that when Richard Layard invited respondents to contextualise their happiness ('how would you say things are these days – would you say you are very happy, pretty happy or not too happy?'), long-term trends suggest that having risen in the 1950s, happiness in the United States has steadily fallen over the following decades, despite the trend towards growing GDP[12]. Equivalent surveys have produced similar results in Europe.[13] It is perhaps the about-face of Swift: 'I asked for riches that I might be happy. I was given poverty that I might be wise.'

Sarkozy's plan fits into this tradition of thought. It, like the Club of Rome's groundbreaking analysis in 1972, explores 'the limits of growth'. It is an argument, too, taken up by *The Spirit Level* using data from our own time, which argues that 'measures of wellbeing and happiness ceased to rise with economic growth but as affluent countries have grown richer, there have been long term rises in... social problems'.[14] The conventional assumption that productivity means happiness is questionable and sits at the heart of this forty year long debate. And yet, by concentrating on wellbeing rather than simply happiness, it is perhaps both more sophisticated in its analysis and more meaningful in its implications for public policy. Nevertheless, it can be said that our collective psychosis relates not to our broad wellbeing but rather to our declining happiness.

Despite the academic analysis, this case for our poor state of happiness is far from absolute, but it is nonetheless compelling. To date though, there is only one country that has embedded the idea of happiness into policy. The government of the

Kingdom of Bhutan in the Himalayas not only measures happiness but considers the impact of each policy decision on 'national happiness'. The result? Were you to visit this small nation, you would not be able to watch wrestling on television.

And there is the cold reality that, as Sorman points out, 'unlike other proposed measures (happiness, for example), economic growth can be determined objectively... Yes, some economists believe it necessary to temper that purely quantitative measurement with such factors as quality of life and efficient management of resources, and there is wide agreement that GDP omits important aspects of economic activity, such as home production. But all economists agree on growth's importance: while a high rate of growth doesn't solve every problem, its absence doesn't solve any.'[15] Real policy making, as can be seen in the response to the credit crunch, must be very wary about harming an economy's capacity for growth. And yet such a parochial drive is somehow left wanting.

One could not put it better than Galbraith who, in his *The Affluent Society* classic, opens with the convincing idea that wealth 'is not without its advantages and the case to the contrary, although it has often been made, has never proved widely persuasive. But, beyond doubt, wealth is the relentless enemy of understanding.'[16]

Nicolas Sarkozy

Perhaps only in France could a President, just months into his term of office, divorce his former model wife (whom he met when he officiated at her wedding in his capacity of Mayor of Neuilly-sur-Seine) only to engage in a very public relationship and marriage barely four months later with singer, song-writer and model Carla Bruni whose previous conquests had included Mick Jagger and Eric Clapton. But the diminutive Sarkozy (reaching a height of 5ft 5) and his most glamorous of first ladies cut quite a figure on the world stage. In many ways, his assault on those '68-ers' was somewhat ironic given Carla's previous relationship with the 'Street Fighting Man' himself, but it is these contradictions which make politics interesting.

Although hailing from the right of French politics (not always the right of international democratic politics), Sarkozy has at times been politically radical. Perhaps only in France 'a kind of luxury Soviet Union' as someone once put it, could this idea of radically challenging the way that economics is valued come from the 'right' of the system. It is all the more astonishing when one considers that these radical ideas are traditionally associated with the most fervent of anti-capitalist economists.[17] But this hyperactive man at the top of French politics has pushed through reforms which have frequently challenged the old elites. His has been something of a Thatcherite, pull yourself up by the bootstraps, attitude. For him, suburban Paris rioters which are almost part of the system of government, are *'racaille'*, he has been tough on immigration, but has also championed social mobility, anti-racism and positive discrimination.

With a Jewish-Hungarian ancestry (although Baptised Catholic), Sarkozy falls outside of the traditional French political background and while he most certainly embraces the rather singular French way of life, perhaps is able to view his country more objectively than some of his predecessors and those around him who were 'bred' to govern. For him, the state is not an ends and is not the only means though this was insufficient to stop him from pouring government funds into the troubled engineering giant Alstom. It seems the instinct to open up markets domestically is not matched by a similar desire to expose French workers to the ravages of global competition.

The New Entitlements

In 2009 the Finish government established a new 'human right' for its citizens. That right was access to broadband and the administration committed €12.5 million to rolling out the technology to its rural communities.[18] There were good reasons behind the initiative which supported the country's claim as a technological pioneer, the knowledge economy and social cohesion. But the idea that broadband should be a human right might have caused many a double take and it feeds into the debate about the appropriate reach of our real entitlements.

To what are we entitled? The General Assembly of the United Nations adopted the Universal Declaration of Human Rights in 1948 as part of the era of international co-operation enjoyed in the aftermath of world war. The signatories committed their countries to entitlements of their citizens ranging from the right to life and liberty to the principle of being innocent until proved guilty to privacy and freedom of movement. It is remarkably detailed, providing for entitlements to education, work, social security and ownership of property.[19] While it has no formal international legal force, the Declaration secured a Guinness World Record entry as the most translated document in the world, appearing in over 300 different language and dialect versions.[20] And it is no coincidence that it appeared in that same post-war period that gave Europe its welfare states and the United States its superpower status; the 'never again' societies of the late 1940s, changed our way of life for good. These were the years which allowed the United States to become an economic and industrial powerhouse, taking advantage of a world in which Europe and Japan, its principle competitors, were rebuilding from the physical devastation of modern war. Michael Moore's otherwise intellectually flimsy film *Capitalism: a love story*,[21] nonetheless points to an unfulfilled dream of President Franklin Roosevelt which draws the entitlement issue into the focus of policy. In his 1944 State of the Union address, and because 'necessitous men are not free men', FDR proposed an 'economic bill of rights' guaranteeing Americans a 'useful and ruminative job'; 'a decent home'; 'a good education'; 'protection from economic fears of old age, sickness, accident and unemployment'; 'the rights of farmers to sell produce at a decent return'; and the rights of business to 'trade free from unfair competition'.[22]

There is a recurring debate, perhaps most prominently played out in the United States, and in both the tabloid and academic circles, which attacks this idea of entitlement. It sees the growth of welfare as synonymous with the growth of selfishness. And despite its implications, it is an idea with both merit and support. Take this tirade, for example, from the controversial, right-wing commentator Glenn Beck whose populist views have made his show on the conservative Fox channel a 'ratings sensation'[23]:

We have raised a generation of would-be killers, the me generation. A generation which only cares about me, me, me, it's mine! A generation we didn't teach the

> *meaning of 'merit'. A generation which doesn't understand what it means to actually earn something because we've handed everything to them... 'we want our healthcare and we want it now'.... That's the lie about Marxism; it's all about the collective, when it's about them.*[24]

That the 'left' can be selfish, even nationalistically so, is without doubt. The debate about EU protectionism in the face of competition from poorer, emerging markets is ultimately a self-interested (as well as misguided) one. It is a proposition which is entirely aimed at safeguarding comfortable European lifestyles against the threat that poorer nations of the world might achieve a degree of redistribution by way of fair economic competition. As the charity Christian Aid has highlighted, the European Union's protectionist Common Agricultural Policy has meant that tomato farmers in the African country of Ghana cannot compete with what should be relatively expensive production in Western Europe. Heavily subsidised EU imports are cheap and have flooded the African market suppressing economic growth and living standards of some of the poorest people on the planet. The story is repeated in different products and different countries.[25] And yet arguments about liberalising economics and trade are associated with the 'right'.

It is the sense of entitlement which pervades. Indeed, one of the perplexities for the self-styled centre left is that voters do not elect them even when it is in their interests due to benefits, programmes or public spending. But it is often that idea that the left (or the state) 'knows what is best for you', which repels support.

But where the polarised argument played out by the conservatives is left wanting is surely not simply that we are selfish and increasingly believe in welfare entitlements, the likes of which those who lived through the 1930s in the West nor indeed those in developing countries today could only have dreamed, but rather that the entitlement generation is not only those at the bottom of the heap; entitlement pervades society. And it does not make us happy.

Opportunity to succeed and build personal and national prosperity is a strength of our free, open and democratic societies. But we believe that we are entitled to become wealthy and harbour the disillusioned notion that the most financially successful amongst us achieved their riches through God given talent alone. One of the reasons for the public row about bankers' bonuses in 2010 and 2011 was not only a tabloid simplistic analysis of a complex crisis but also one which responded to the insensitivities of those in high paying jobs who felt entitled to even greater pay. While bank bonuses were effectively being subsidised by British, European and American taxpayers, those in potential receipt acted with a glaring insensitivity. Such attitudes were acknowledged by Barclays boss, John Varley in a *New Statesman* interview when he told Mehdi Hasan:

> *...the banking industry got a lot of things wrong. As a chief executive of a big bank, I acknowledge that and am grateful that governments, through the injection of taxpayers' money, rescued the global banking system... I have to be sensitive to what the public thinks, because a lot of taxpayers' money has been put to work in the banking system. And if the pay of nurses and teachers is*

> *frozen because of the economic crisis, then the public is going to look carefully at what bankers get paid... But pay judgements are difficult. I am obliged, as chief executive, to field the very best people I can by paying fairly. But be clear - we're seeking to pay the minimum consistent with remaining competitive.*[26]

That minimum consistent with remaining competitive, it turned out just a few weeks later, was a record breaking payment of some £2.3bn to Barclays investment bankers celebrating record profits.[27] The point is not so much the great wealth given the context but rather the sense of entitlement; a sense of outrage in the banking community about being denied their bonuses which equalled the outrage in civil society about them being paid. There was a very real fear in London and Wall Street about the consequences of unilateral government action to curb pay by way of regulation and taxation. In an ever globalised world, these two great financial centres looked vulnerable to business moving to Switzerland, Singapore, Hong Kong or even China. Such moves, were they to occur, would not be driven by corporate mission but rather by demands of employees to be paid what they believe to be their entitlement.

It can be seen in the salaries which directors of quoted companies frequently award themselves. In the ten years from 1994 to 2004 (pre-credit crunch) the median pay of FTSE 100 CEOs grew by a staggering 92% to £579,000.[28] In the post recession 'austerity' year of 2010, FTSE 100 director pay went up 55%, awarding the average CEO an annual package of £4.9 million a year.[29] It is because 'they are worth it'.

There can be few more powerful refutations of this notion than the view put forthrightly by the sometime richest man on the planet. Billionaire investor Warren Buffett openly accepts that his talents are limited. Cited by no less a writer than Barak Obama he says, 'I happen to have a talent for allocating capital. But my ability to use that talent is completely dependent on the society I was born into. If I'd been born into a tribe of hunters, this talent of mine would be pretty worthless. I can't run very fast. I'm not particularly strong. I'd probably end up as some wild animal's dinner'.[30] It is a magnanimous attitude towards the debt the wealthy West owes to its society which is not shared by many people many times less rich than Buffett who look only to their entitlements.

In one very real way a sense of entitlement at the bottom of society to be looked after has preserved that at the very top of society to own and to govern. Entitlement is responsible for the preservation of elites and general unfairness within and between countries. It also breeds profligate behaviour since actions become (personally at least) without consequence. In the pursuit of riches our entitlements have extended to that of pollution; the environment is ours to use as we like. We feel an entitlement to burn fuel and to consume protein at a pace which is unsustainable if replicated by the rest of the planet (as it increasingly is). The irony is that our riches and the entitlements that these bring have not served to make our societies happy or more content.

Harvard University's Grant Group and Oxford's Toby Ord

The commitment of 268 onetime Harvard undergraduates to further the study of just what makes us happy knows no ends it seems; some have even donated their brains. This elite group of men known as the 'Grant Group', who arrived at the college just before the Second World War, and rumoured to include future President John F. Kennedy, were to take part in a truly ambitious longitudinal research project which continues until this day. Indeed, the study has been extended to include some 824 men and women over the course of their lives. Its conclusion, some three score years and ten after it began, 'being rich doesn't make you happy; being nice does.'[31]

The young Oxford philosophy academic Toby Ord created a fair amount of press attention in the autumn of 2009 when, this modestly paid man, pledged to donate over a third of his £33,000 salary to charities fighting poverty in the developing world in addition to a further 10% of his earnings for the rest of his working life for what he plans will amount to a million pounds to charity over his career. He told journalists at *The Telegraph*, 'the things I gain most from – spending time with my wife, with friends, listening to beautiful music, reading beautiful books – don't cost money'.[32] Ord, not a rich man by European or North American standards, is nonetheless wealthy by comparison to some of the poorest corners of the world. But like the findings from the Grant Group, he believes that being nice in this way makes him happy. Founding the organisation *Giving What We Can*, to promote the idea of donating ten percent of income, Ord argued that a person earning just £15,000 per year could save 55 lives a year and that 'far from making their lives miserable, members say that taking the Pledge to Give has made their lives happier and more fulfilled.'[33]

Decline of Class Identification

For most people, the desire to accumulate is a natural and understandable disposition. And while the elites, plus those at the very bottom of the heap and perhaps all of the rest of us in between in our own way, continue to pervade our societies with that sense of entitlement in plain view, the developed world today is more meritocratic. As a consequence, the measuring stick of success dovetails with the focus of policy: wealth creation. It is perhaps this need to identify and to be identified in terms of our relative wealth status that has led to products such as the Apple iPhone app 'I am Rich'. Selling for $999 in the Apple Stores, the application (which was removed from sale after just a day) did nothing more than glow red with the option of displaying the text 'I am rich, I deserve it, I am good, healthy & successful' (sic), when the button was pressed. Eight people bought it: six from the US, and one each from Germany and France.[34] This is surely the most modern and most indulgent incarnation of the Gold/Platinum/Black credit card or even vanity number plates (but without entertaining others) each merely a display of wealth; a signal to others that we have accumulated riches; not a signal that we are happy or content. 'In rich countries, it is now the symbolic importance of wealth and possessions that matters. What purchases say about status and identity is often more important than the goods themselves.'[35] It is all part of the narrowing of our destiny and is something which President Jimmy Carter warned Americans about as the energy crisis bit in 1979:

Human identity is no longer defined by what one does, but by what one owns. But we've discovered that owning things and consuming things does not satisfy our longing for meaning. We've learned that piling up material goods cannot fill the emptiness of lives which have no confidence or purpose.[36]

As our societies have become more meritocratic (though social mobility remains stilted) we derive our status less by our traditional idea of class than by our possessions – and all the more so without a coherent idea of just what the wealth is for. To a significant extent, status was always supported by wealth since the Nouveau Riche can join the higher classes within a generation or so and likewise the upper class family which becomes destitute will in all likelihood find themselves slipping in social status. Class was never a satisfactory system and was rarely practiced in the States as it was in Europe. But like never before it is now wealth and possessions that define us. Society celebrates the vacuous but financially successful (the 'glamour model Katie 'Jordan' Price sold the best part of half a million copies of three different autobiographies by the age of 32); and promotes the idea of instant success and entitlement. In doing so, we perhaps fail to value community, education, thought, culture and genuine fulfilment. These things, after all, were amongst the ambitions of the 1950s futurologists when they conjured visions of the future and our present.

In the society we have built, one has to be much more sophisticated to access 'happiness'. Complex, multi-layered societies compare starkly in this respect to ones where people are 'just surviving'. It explains why we gravitate both towards the crudeness of meaningless materialism and even the refined liberal arts access to a level of emotion is lost from our everyday lives.

Life, Liberty and the Pursuit of Riches?

Strangely, the idea of our happiness and quality of life is an objective of the European Union and United States alike. In the creation of these polities their 'founding fathers' enshrined happiness rather than wealth into their very beings. Perhaps the most famous line from the United States Declaration of Independence is the right to 'life, liberty and the pursuit of happiness.' It is an unalienable right which drew philosophically from John Locke. In the protracted row which was the EU's Berlin Declaration, signatories agreed to be united 'zu unserem Gluck' in the German version, or 'in happiness' as might be translated. Fearing the emotiveness, English versions watered down the language to read united 'for the common good.'[37] But nonetheless, the idea of wellbeing or straightforward happiness, is a core visionary objective of American and European politics. While the freedom guarantees wealth creation and commercial life as we know it, politically (and indeed constitutionally) this simpler idea remains at its core. But it is the pursuit of riches which has characterised our implementation of this power. Making the world safe for capitalism is a far more accurate description of the wealthy West's projection of power despite earlier, loftier, aims.

Eleanor Roosevelt had supported the Universal Declaration of Human Rights (rather than a Treaty) so that it had the same influence on societies across the world that the US constitution had on America. It was not to be a dusty agreement but rather a living document owned by all. President Roosevelet's own 'second bill of rights' reminds one more of the EEC in its protection of farmers, welfare and the free movement of goods and people than that envisaged by the founding fathers. Indeed FDR's plan, had it come into being, would not have altered the US constitution in any way. But it all represents a real intent; a broader and positive vision of what our riches can do to improve lives, help those most in need and promote happiness. If we are to realise ambitions of forming a political strand to the mixed economic settlement, we must try to reach back to these ideals.

Eleanor Roosevelt

Born into the great wealth and corresponding privilege of late nineteenth century high society New York, Eleanor Roosevelt would nonetheless become a prominent advocate for civil rights and equality. Politics and power were in the blood. At 17 she began a relationship with her fifth cousin once removed, Franklin D. Roosevelt, the man who was to become her husband and later US President. This followed a White House function hosted by her uncle, President Theodore Roosevelt. For all the power around her though, she busied herself as volunteer in the slums along the East Side of the great city she called home.

Eleanor took a more prominent role in politics as her husband's career progressed, often taking his place when incapacitated following an illness which left him paralysed. But she was also a great supporter of workers' and children's rights and fundraised for the Women's Trade Union League during the 1920s while simultaneously assuming a presence in the Democratic Party.

In 1933 she became First Lady as FDR swapped the New York Governor's mansion for the White House. Eleanor can lay claim to being the first independent First Lady, establishing a weekly press conference and challenging schedule of her own. Men, of course, were banned from these, a bequest to female journalists. During twelve years in office, she supported workers and was outspoken on the need for black and minority rights even appointing the black civil rights leader, Mary McLeod Bethune, as a key adviser. But it was to be many more years, and after her own death, before segregation came to an end.

President Roosevelt died at the end of war in 1945. Shortly afterwards, his successor Harry Truman appointed Eleanor Roosevelt as a delegate to the new United Nations General Assembly where she helped draft the declaration on Human Rights and campaigned actively for its work. She was a familiar figure in post-war America, writing, speaking and broadcasting. Later, the young President Kennedy appointed her Chair of the Presidential Commission on the Status of Women whose forthright conclusions of the need to recognise gender differences were published shortly after her death in 1962.

Something Happiness Cannot Buy

The danger with the happiness argument is its logical conclusion; an outcome which might well converge with the more simplistic ideal of generating economic growth and wealth: hedonism and excess. Happiness economics, Toby Ord and the proponents of entitlement idealise the simple pleasures of humanity but given the opportunity of policy aimed at fulfilling happiness, society is capable of turning its back on altruism in favour of socially, as well as economically unproductive activities. Conversely, those proponents of prioritising growth and open markets were somewhat removed from the world of greed, excess and selfishness that their policies were said to represent.

Happiness economists today would quite naturally position themselves as counter to the market fundamentalism of Thatcherism and Reaganomics and yet the two polar positions ultimately share the idealistic promotion of self-interest and potentially the unintended policy consequence of societal activities at variance with their own ideas of personal behaviour. Rarely has there been a more straightforward statement of public policy intent than Margaret Thatcher's own early retrospective on her programme in office:

> *I came to office with one deliberate intent. To change Britain from a dependent to a self-reliant society – from a give-it-to-me to a do-it-yourself nation; to a get-up-and-go instead of a sit-back-and-wait-for-it Britain.*[38]

Speaking to the Small Business Bureau in 1984 she empathised with being 'on the go all the time' since she had been brought up in a small business and being prime minister meant 'living above the shop' at Number Ten. Thatcher's dream was of the enterprise culture; individuals forging their own way through life with success being the reward of hard work. While personally wealthy, the result of careful marriage, her Methodist upbringing and puritanical attitudes nonetheless meant that Thatcher eschewed the luxuries of riches and the privileges of leisure which they bring, in favour of hard work and constant work. Known to get by on just four hours sleep a night, she revelled in the cramped work conditions of Downing Street where during the Falklands conflict she stayed up all night heated only by a two bar electric fire and a glass of whisky.[39]

But the society she created during the 1980s was one which became caricatured by excess and for those who benefited most from her policies, hedonism. Rarely is there a television account of the decade which is not accompanied by worn archive footage of big bespectacled, big haired, braces wearing *yuppies*, downing champagne in a City bar. Their lives were organised by *filofax*, they spoke on mobile telephones the size of bricks and they drove ostentatious Porsche 911 turbos with outlandish spoilers and personalised number plates. The caricature does not accurately reflect the real lives of most people in Britain (or elsewhere) during the period. The country was divided and there was hardship for some. For the many, the period offered opportunities to get on the housing ladder, to invest in shares and to enjoy professional freedoms as well as threats to their way of life by way of deindustrialisation and the fragmentation of society. But for those whose mobility was most successfully transformed by the economic and social policies of the Thatcher government, for those who took the most advantage of her belief in 'get-up-and-go', easy credit and meritocracy the end result was seen as individualism and selfish excess. The caricatures of the era would not have been the type of company with which Thatcher herself would have felt comfortable nor indeed would have sought.

The critique of traditionally growth focussed economics, the idea as Keynes put it, that 'avarice and usury must be our gods for a little longer still'[40] is difficult to ignore. But the idea that policy should be focussed narrowly on happiness is equally perplexing. Indeed, the end result might not be too different if more equally dispersed. Immorality, after all, can make us happy.

Making the world a better place

What then are the implication for public policy? Simple hedonistic happiness should not be the ambition of policy. Stiglitz and Sen argue as much in their inclusion of sustainability. But policy directed towards improving lives and (lofty as it sounds) the world might seem more appropriate than one aimed at merely increasing consumption. It is a point made in the report when it argues flippantly that 'Traffic jams may increase GDP as a result of the increased use of gasoline, but obviously not the quality of life. Moreover, if citizens are concerned about the quality of air, and air pollution is increasing, then statistical measures which ignore air pollution will provide an inaccurate estimate of what is happening to citizens' well-being. Or a tendency to measure gradual change may be inadequate to capture risks of abrupt alterations in the environment such as climate change'.[41] Politics need to do more than simply build these aims into policy, however, when it can rediscover genuine visions of a better world from within our very own constitutional systems.

There is a more personal reality of what Matthew Crawford calls 'infantilisation'. It is the proposal that our modern societies have less opportunities to do, to make or for people to see their impact on the world leading to a sense of dependence rather than the self-reliance we crave. The harsh truth of globalisation has meant that policy has focussed on 'the knowledge economy' but Crawford argues the trend has been misguided as people no longer can see what it is that they achieve. 'There is nothing new about American futurism. What is new is the wedding of futurism to what might be called 'virtualism': a vision of the future in which we somehow take leave of material reality and glide about in a pure information economy.'[42] The rediscovery of individual and collective purpose is central to reversing the two decade long trend.

As politics becomes more difficult, policy objectives will have to be relocated not simply in enabling economic growth and wastefulness but rather in a longer term appreciation of sustainable society. This means a concept of wellbeing that is more sophisticated than hedonistic happiness; which has sustainability that goes beyond the simple idea of ecological protection; and an economy from which people can once again derive worth. The good news is, this is within the capability of capitalist economics.

Chapter Eight

Hardship and Rejuvenation

As the credit crunched in 2008, signalling the end of a binge decade which saw consumption grow at a pace to embarrass even the high rollers of the 1980s, there was a moment where our developed societies might have done things just a little differently. There was just a brief moment of clarity when, like Rhomer's *Green Ray*, people saw the folly of their excess and politics renewed its belief in government. Alas, it was short-lived. Markets reasserted their authority over the state and the solution to a downturn in part caused by excessive consumer spending was more of the same.

It was a perfect example of Keynes' 'paradox of thrift' where it is in society's interest for everyone to spend but in the individuals' interest to save. Government encouraged spending and in doing so revived the markets. But that should not mean that, in recovery, in the second decade, policy, society, politics and economics are not done, just a little, differently. Solutions must be sought to the most wicked of problems and we must demand the development of a political strand to the mixed economic settlement to complete and hold together the project. Fundamentally, we need to broaden the ambitions for our future capitalist societies.

Periods of hardship often make us want to do things differently. Indeed, the mixed economic settlement is predicated, to some degree, on this truth. It is to some degree the motivation for the punctuated equilibrium in the long sweep of policy making. After all, it was the clash, sorrow and destruction of war which prompted the 'never again' generation to back the Beveridge plan; it was a mix of racial subjugation and societal repression which forged the social liberalism of the sixties and policy failure combined with economic decline which sparked the belief in self-interested markets during the 1980s and the collapse of communism which saw it spread to the East.

The economic downturn which followed the banking crisis was the most severe since the great depression of the 1930s and was truly global in its reach. But it was perhaps that severity which ultimately prevented post-crisis reform from being any more rejuvenating than necessary structural change. The fact is that at the London summit in April 2009, world leaders really did fear that our system of capital could collapse and that this second decade of the twenty first century would be a Japanese style lost decade at best; as bleak as the 1930s at worst. President Harry Truman once remarked that 'it's a recession when your neighbour loses his job. Depression is when you lose yours'. The reality of this downturn too is that while most people were aware that they were experiencing a recession, public policy cushioned people in their everyday lives from the very worst of its effects. So the economy shrank, but it recovered in months not years; unemployment rose, but not as high as economists had predicted. That movement was perhaps lost as the true severity was obscured by the effects of public policy which propped up the system. But the after effects

210

would be felt into the second decade, with recovery proving to be as difficult as recession itself. The cost for many countries was a burgeoning budget deficit and for many people caution and belt tightening. The Eurozone had to contend with the ill effects of the poor budget management of the so called PIGS countries (Portugal, Italy, Greece, and Spain) whose loose fiscal management of a decade came back to haunt the single currency project. Warren Buffett put it more succinctly: 'it's only when the tide goes out that you can see who's been swimming naked'. The change in attitude for politicians was for a time, and palpably, more solidarity and confidence in the role of the state, if also a realisation that resources to support that role were depleted. But the experience of most people going about their lives means that the credit crunch represented a missed opportunity to rejuvenate priorities of societies everywhere.

In the aftermath of recession, there was indeed a payback time. Payback not simply for the billions pumped into the global economy after the credit crunch, and which will be reviewed in this chapter, but a natural payback for over-revving capitalism; a payback for that single-minded pursuit of riches. The economic crisis was not simply a story of banking excess, it was the consequence of our riches, our comfortable lives and our wicked demands for public spending and low taxation. We all have to pay and while some are more culpable than others, there is little point in trying to figure who was most to blame or who was left standing when the music stopped.

This chapter looks optimistically to the future from the illuminating position of policy making in the decade after the crisis. It looks to our fragile environment and the next phase of industrialisation, it argues that for politics to renew it needs to address properly the idea of fairness and, having held its own futurology symposium, offers a way forward towards completing the project of the mixed economic settlement. But it represents only part of the means, not the ends.

Dealing with the Crisis

One should not underestimate either the severity of the economic crisis which began in 2008 or indeed the endurance of the mixed economic settlement (or at least the political product of it) in stepping in to tackle the crunch. As President Bush put is so memorably at the time, 'this sucker could go down'. The 'sucker' was the global economy. As the banking system crumbled, governments in the US and Europe put their hands into very deep pockets and nationalised very big banks. This was a time when capitalists in the most capitalist country in the world, with arguably the most capitalist of presidents sitting in the White House acquiesced to huge state intervention in the economy. The pragmatism of the mixed economic settlement to maintain capitalism was apparent and it was remarkable that as Fannie Mae and Freddie Mac were taken into state ownership, the markets, as represented by the Dow Jones and its many partners across the globe, rallied. By way of comparison, when, a week later, President Bush's administration declined to save Lehman Brothers, despite pleas from a family employee to step in, equity valuations slumped at the idea of the bank's fate being left to the market.[1]

If even the market was cheering the actions of the state, was anyone prepared to defend the idea of market fundamentalism? After all, the mixed economic settlement embodied the idea that the market was always right. There were just a handful of

US House Representatives upholding the market ideal when the $700 billion toxic loan banks bail out was debated in October of 2008. Texas Republican, Rep. Jeb Hensarling, argued before the House that the United States should not reject its free-market principles and begin along what he called the 'slippery slope to socialism,' adding reasonably, 'how can we have capitalism on the way up, and socialism on the way down?'[2] It might have been an argument made equally passionately by the extreme left many of whom saw the banking crisis as a long awaited collapse of capitalism.

It is instructive for observers of the mixed economic settlement that while the extremes of view both left and right, rejected the package to 'save capitalism' with state intervention, mainstream political opinion right across the world lined up in its support. And the effect of that support, that global coordination, was a shorter, perhaps sharper, shock than might otherwise have been the case. Economic disruption for sure, followed by years of dealing with the public finance consequences, was the result. But it also meant preservation, indeed even a strengthening, of the mixed economic settlement as it had come to be. Gordon Brown's Freudian slip to the Commons that he had 'saved the world' gave confidence to politicians that they were indeed right. This despite the truth that Brown's own record of economic stewardship was not only partially culpable for the crisis but also the principles by which he had managed British public finances for ten years – the golden rule – were unceremoniously thrown out of the Treasury's back window overnight. Ironically it showed that the state does not always know best.

The focus of dealing with the crisis was single minded: growth, growth, growth. Few politicians speak more eloquently than President Obama whose uplifting speech to a joint session of Congress told his country:

> *While our economy may be weakened and our confidence shaken; though we are living through difficult and uncertain times, tonight I want every American to know this: We will rebuild, we will recover, and the United States of America will emerge stronger than before. The weight of this crisis will not determine the destiny of this nation. The answers to our problems don't lie beyond our reach... we have lived through an era where too often, short-term gains were prized over long-term prosperity; where we failed to look beyond the next payment, the next quarter, or the next election....*
>
> *The recovery plan and the financial stability plan are the immediate steps we're taking to revive our economy in the short-term. But the only way to fully restore America's economic strength is to make the long-term investments that will lead to new jobs, new industries, and a renewed ability to compete with the rest of the world.[3]*

The speech is notable for acknowledging many of the tragedies of our riches; the short-termism, competition states and a singular belief in prosperity. But it has a clear focus on 'doing whatever proves necessary' to stimulate economic growth. And so the message rang out very clear: growth remains the focus of public policy.

Opportunities Missed, Redeploying Capitalism

The rescue with all that it entailed was necessary to protect the global economy; it was necessary to safeguard our wealth, prosperity, services and even our way of life. And while recession meant a permanent loss of output and the world emerged from downturn poorer than it had entered, the crisis represented a shock rather than an epiphany. Some things will doubtless be done differently in the second decade and we should ensure that policy makers and investors alike are more sensitive to the dangers of asset bubbles. But in the immediate aftermath, with the emphasis very firmly on re-establishing growth, ambitions to redeploy our great riches in the direction of a broader destiny appeared rather thin. There were, however, still reasons to be hopeful. And if only to show how short our memories, it is worth considering the economist L.M. Holt who presented a paper entitled *Panics and Booms* to the Southern California Editorial Association in 1897. His words are prescient today:

Good times will follow bad times, and bad times will follow good times just as surely as darkness follows day, and day follows darkness. These periods always have followed each other and they always will. The seeds of prosperity are sown during the periods of financial depression, and the seeds of hard times are just as surely sown during the period of business activity and the speculative boom. There is no question as to the soundness of this conclusion. There is no question that these changes will come. The only question is, when?

215

At the close of a speculative boom the change comes like a thief in the night. In fact a thief in the night would be a welcome visitor to many instead of the change which puts in an appearance, but the change from a financial depression to better times comes gradually, so gradually that for months there is a difference of opinion as to whether a change for the better has actually commenced or not.[4]

It is a telling commentary on events to occur more than a century later. The question for politics and for society is, what sort of prosperity do we want as the change from financial depression to better times comes? What will be our new vision for a future capitalist world? There is, of course, stability and in reaching back to a sage of old, one might etch the following words of J.K. Galbraith into the walls of policy makers, analysts, investors and commentators. A chronicler of the 1929 Wall Street crash, he warned back in 1961, 'someday, no one can tell when, there will be another speculative climax and crash. There is no chance that, as the market moves to the brink, those involved will see the nature of the illusion and so protect themselves and the system. The mad can communicate their madness; they cannot perceive it and resolve to be sane.'[5] If only we had listened.

Policy makers have reacted to the credit crunch in such a way that there will not be another banking bubble tomorrow. But then, having just experienced one, there was never going to be. There is little likelihood that by the time the banks experience another bubble, a possibility far in the future, that the new regulations put into place after 2009 will still exist in quite the same form. The truth is that human beings are apt to create asset bubbles which from only a short distance appear absurd. After all, if the tech bubble of the late 1990s is not incongruous enough, remember that in the seventeenth century there was a bubble no less intense over tulips. It is perhaps that very human nature which permits bubbles which also must accept some responsibility for our accumulative nature discussed in these pages. In being more aware about bubbles and market imperfections, our economic lives might just be more sophisticated. But market imperfections should not automatically mean more state interference. Dealing with externalities and issues of public goods will often require government but the state alone is a poor substitute for sustainable partnerships capable of riding out the short-term vagaries of party politics and tribalism.

Before the banking bubble burst there were some efforts to manoeuvre policy towards tackling climate change and as the crisis took hold, there was a moment when society looked in on itself and saw the tragedy of our riches. But the intensification of policy aims towards re-establishing growth, a necessary focus given both the circumstances and the embeddedness of the mixed economic settlement, meant that these faded.

The challenge, if politics is willing to accept, is in redeploying capitalism into a mission which is more cavernous than just growth. It is about creating a richness to life, society and every day experience. It is about accepting the need to improve wellbeing not just wealth. It is about using those riches to 'buy' time that does more than offer leisure, but allows family, community, knowledge, thought and culture to prosper. There are perennial Western issues here of lifestyle and work life balance. But this cannot be about contract terms with an employer, it must be a new contract with our society.

217

This surely is reflected in some of those ambitions from the futurologists of the 1950s before our destiny became limited. They need to be recaptured.

The long term pursuit of growth, crash and recession has meant we had payback time to get things back on track. It is important that we accept this is true of our broader economy experience. There is always a payback for excess and success. The baby boom generation might have enjoyed 'something for nothing' in its consumption of the world's resources, but in the second decade of the twenty first century we really are paying for those years. There are wicked problems, the most prominent of which is the environment which has been damaged by humankind. Again we have to accept payback. And once we do, it is possible to see the political economy as a more cohesive entity where the deployment of our riches can be more fulfilling.

Next Phase of Industrialisation

Regardless of the continuity, the economic crisis and the emergence from it put the future sharply into focus. It was a future in which the emerging nations of the world, led by the mighty China, would play an increasingly important role and one where as these economies industrialise, the mature economies of the West seek to establish a new phase in their own development.

Deindustrialisation in Europe and the United States has been blamed for many of the financial ills of our age whether it is inequalities or long-term unemployment. Its onset in the 1980s after a decade of economic and industrial decline marked the very final nail in the coffin of the golden age of capitalism.

Traditional industrial and manufacturing output and jobs declined, replaced by a thriving service economy. Countries which endured the harshest of monetarist policies, under Thatcherism and Reaganomics, suffered the greatest decline in traditional industries. While Germany clung on to its car manufacturing sector, for instance, Britain's one time 'motown' in Coventry all but disappeared. According to the Office for National Statistics, at end of the Second World War, British manufacturing represented some 40% of the economy, by the new millennium it was a declining 20%. While the process of deindustrialisation represented real hardship (and unnatural shocks can decimate otherwise healthy business), there is also a compelling argument which says that it can be a positive feature of a developed economy and reflective of earlier moves to industrialise now replicated across these emerging economies of the world.

The German economist, Ernst Engel, observed a reality of economic development and living standards. Engel's law stated simply that as income rises, the proportion of our wealth spent on food declines. More disposable income means increased demand for manufactured goods. Meanwhile, supply is increased as technological advancement means that agricultural production requires less labour. As such, industrialisation occurs with migration from the land to the cities and such a phenomenon happened in Europe during the industrial revolution in the eighteenth and nineteenth centuries just as it has happened and continues to occur in the China led East in recent years and today. Similarly, the case can be made deindustrialisation is the phase where an economy moves from manufacturing to services. Indeed some Asian economies appear to have already begun such a transition on a road paved by Europe and the USA. Just as technological advancement allowed for more efficient agricultural production then so too can innovation mean that productivity in manufacturing grows more fervently than that of services and it is the service sector whose workforce expands to keep pace with industrial output. The case has been made no less powerfully and yet pragmatically than Rowthorn and Ramswamy in their 1997 IMF working paper. They state bluntly that deindustrialisation 'is not a negative phenomenon in its own right. It is an unenviable feature of economic development, predating the emergence of both rising inequality and unemployment in advanced economies.... Deindustrialisation is primarily a feature of successful economic development.'[6]

The service sector which emerged from the 1980s has been dominated (especially in Britain) by financial services and the handful of big banks which brought the world to its economic knees in 2008. The continued and single-minded focus on economic growth has had implications for the environment. And we have enjoyed prosperity without a clear idea as to why we were creating it.

The banking crisis hit economies right across the world. But the impact on Britain showed up the great imbalances in the UK economy which had become so reliant on banking and financial services. Britain was far more exposed to the crisis, at least proportionally, than many of its European allies or even the United States where the crunch began. Since the so called 'big bang' de-regulation in 1986 the City of London's financial services industry boomed just as traditional industry declined. It was a huge success, creating riches for a generation, not to mention innovation and a top notch 'knowledge economy'. The Blair-Brown governments saw it as an easy 'cash cow' which they milked for a decade of increased public spending. That New Labour government was sanguine about wealth epitomised by Peter Mandelson's famous decree that he was 'intensely relaxed about people getting filthy rich'. Brown's Treasury bragged about Britain's 'light touch regulation' - lighter even than that of Wall Street. The result was a sector which boomed, able to absorb shocks such as the tech bubble and becoming essential to the prosperity of the broader economy.

But it created economic imbalances which seemed only to dawn on British policy makers in the wake of the crisis. While there were those who irresponsibly argued for a deliberate shrinking of British financial services, there emerged a mainstream consensus for the need to rebuild alternative industrial sectors. It is a view shared across the developed and developing world and will surely shape the industrial mix of this young decade. Ironically, the City itself along with Wall Street are likely to finance this vision.

The history of government 'picking winners' in industry, is a poor one. It reached its height and nadir simultaneously in the 1970s after which the idea of economic intervention declined. While some in the trade unions have provided lone voices favouring a return to a British industrial past, a cherished golden age as it were, this is not what is on offer today.

A commitment to green technology is a vision shared across the political divide in Britain, Europe and the United States. Both the incoming coalition and outgoing UK Labour governments were at one on this. In his final Budget as Chancellor, Alistair Darling confirmed this new tack combined with greater state involvement and encouraging a balanced economy:

221

The role of modern government is to work with the key sectors to help them compete and prosper. We will not go back to the interventionism of the past. But nor can we return to the hands-off approach of the free-marketeers.[7]

Governments across the world have agreed to climate change targets and in this new decade, policy will have to deliver on those commitments. With green infrastructure and transport at its heart, capital spending also creates growth. The plan is not without its detractors. The environmentalist George Mombiot has questioned the economic case with the point that while public transport is cleaner, rail expansion which stimulates growth inevitably means more people travelling each and every day. 'Why the assumption that transport networks will grow and grow forever?', he asks.[8]

Nevertheless, green technology is the beginnings of a policy which itself just begins to square one of the wicked problems of politics. In itself it is only a first step and on its own it is woefully insufficient. It cannot be used to allow continued collusion between politician and voter in the fiction that climate change can be dealt with without substantial changes in behaviour. We still need to burn less. It is crucial that the societal and global sides of the programme are fulfilled too. But that can only happen with a sea change in the way we do politics, debate the issues and interact with the state. We need to face up to what we mean by fairness at home in our rich societies and abroad where people are less fortunate. The consensus achieved in politics here needs to be extended into more challenging and difficult environmental policy but it also needs to be replicated in other policy areas, driven down into stable partnerships in society or indeed up from communities into government.

Fairness Agenda and the Cheat

As a political statement, 'fairness' can be interpreted as vacuous since it difficult to disagree with the slogan. Who genuinely believes that policy should be more unfair as a matter of principle? Most certainly there are those who accept unfairness but it is not the intrinsic motivation. And yet fairness has gathered ground as an agenda for democratic politics. The question is reduced to whose fairness? We have tended towards a warped utilitarian notion of fairness even. Fairness for the majority is not always fair and even with a dose of deontology with roles and duties which sit above this, policymaking is left wanting in our polity of the unsustainable cheat, where the irreconcilable is promised and accepted. Rejuvenating politics has to be about fairness not simply efficiency and we are going to have to understand the notion properly. But this is not simply the philosophical clash of the libertarian position of say taxation being theft versus the Marxist take on property as similarly stealing. The philosopher Robert Nozick is perhaps the most prominent proponent of the former. The French sometime anarchist, socialist, politician cum philosopher Pierre-Joseph Proudhon personifies the latter. If we are interested in 'fairness', presented are two irreconcilable positions. The most famous of quotations from Proudhon's *What is Property?* puts the case starkly:

> *If I were asked to answer the following question: What is slavery? and I should answer in one word, it is*

223

murder. My meaning would be understood at once. No extended argument would be required . . . Why, then, to this other question: What is property? may I not likewise answer, It is robbery, without the certainty of being misunderstood; the second proposition being no other than a transformation of the first?[9]

The counter is no less forceful. Contrast this with Nozick's controversial view about income tax:

Taxation of earnings from labour is on a par with forced labour. Some persons find this claim obviously true: taking the earnings of n hours labour is like taking n hours from the person; it is like forcing the person to work n hours for another's purpose. Others find the claim absurd. But even these, if they object to forced labour, would oppose forcing unemployed hippies to work for the benefit of the needy. And they would also object to forcing each person to work five extra hours each week for the benefit of the needy.[10]

The point is that each position believes itself to be expressing ultimate fairness. Alas the positions contradict demonstrating the futility of fairness as a programme as we have come to understand it through manifesto pledges and political rhetoric. But this big argument does not help to reconcile the real demand for 'fairness' in democratic, policy development. This is perhaps because, as an agenda, fairness is about juggling and balancing the mixed economic settlement but it must do so in a much harsher, more global, world. It is a much narrower and more focused proposition than the great philosophical debates which cannot be satisfied. In seeking fairness in mainstream policy, it seems unlikely that the argument will ever be fully reconciled either but that does not make it any less legitimate. There is the need to tear apart false tribalism and push decisions away from simple utilitarianism and further towards post majoritarian politics.

Here we might draw on the great modern thinker, John Rawls, whose *Theory of Justice* is explicit in its case for 'fairness'. Rawls proposed the powerful idea of a 'veil of ignorance' through which issues can be examined morally. That is one has to imagine that societal roles have been redistributed and we do not know the role to which we have been assigned. So we do not know our wealth, social standing, ability or intelligence. For Rawls, 'if a knowledge of particulars is allowed, then the outcome is biased by arbitrary contingency'.[11] In tackling fairness and the great wicked problems of policy, the concept of a veil of ignorance is not only useful, it is essential.

Fairness in the mixed economic settlement is a response to the unsustainable cheat outlined in a previous chapter. The three liberal constituents of the settlement are not fixed. Their influence and prioritisation remain in constant flux with policy movement creating winners and losers who might identify in a less extreme way with the positions of Nozick or Proudhon. The debate in the United States over healthcare reform encapsulates the debate perfectly. It is about addressing the impossible question 'whose fairness?' And it is about asking for sacrifices and using the great economic power of our developed economies to achieve a broader vision. But the outcome of the flux was to extend healthcare just as the outcome in Germany was to draw back on the reach of the welfare state. Fairness, after all, is an agenda item of the traditional right and the traditional left and can be observed in the popular movements of campaigning charities such as Oxfam and the Tea Party movement in the USA.

Wider than our own societies though, we have to countenance the great challenge that if 'the world is flat' or at least becoming flatter, then the rich must be fair to the poorest of the world and that means exposing our wealth to greater risk. The globalised world we have helped create over the years since the Second World War has undoubtedly limited our independent ability to form policy. But it has also allowed Europe and the United States, along with the rest of the developed world, to become very rich. Free market ideology was foisted upon fragile emerging economies which are now competing with our fatter welfare states. The rhetoric from the EU and no less strongly echoed by American politicians is to draw up the bridge and build protectionist barriers around our rich, comfortable world and refuse to trade on equal terms or indeed on the terms our own governments insisted were adhered to by the poorest of the world. Our position is selfish and most certainly unfair. But will we have the courage to risk some of our great wealth for this greater good?

Fairness, then, is a legitimate political agenda and it can be identified across major global developed economies spurred on by the inequities displayed during the credit crunch. After all, was it fair that low income taxpayers had to support the richest banks in the world as they teetered on the edge of collapse? Is it fair that the richest are able to legally avoid taxation and as Buffett points out 'pay less as a percentage of their income than their secretaries'? Is it fair that large corporations can undermine their workers? Is it fair that some people in society *choose* not to work but are supported nonetheless by the state? Is it fair that the richest countries in the world want to protect themselves from the competition from the poorest? These are difficult questions and we have to accept that we cannot always have both sides of a wicked problem.

Civic Renewal

The idea of civic renewal is not new but it has become more pressing. Such ideas go back to Hobbes. Locke and Mill. During the Clinton presidency, numerous civic partnerships emerged such as the Civic Practices Network to help government meet citizens' needs. And in Britain the National Council for Voluntary Organisations engaged in the civil renewal debate as 'a vision of what society should look like; it is about ideals and goals.'[12] Indeed the British Home Office even created a forgotten Civil Renewal Unit in 2004. But today, renewal is needed in order that society can prioritise collective needs.

State, cultural, neighbourhood and societal renewal must be part of this but the ownership is also what matters. Politics cannot remain as something done to us or else there is little incentive for communities or individuals to mobilise. And such civic politics needs to be about more than the political economy and as much about our immediate environment and the opportunity (indeed the expectation) to learn and to develop. It is these very questions that will be considered in the months following the August 2011 riots in London and across English cities.

Civic renewal also needs to ignore distinctions between the state, the individual, the market, private organised capital and social enterprise. After all these surely overlap and individuals who form society are stakeholders in multiple areas. That is not to say, however, that civic society can ever be a substitute for the state tackling the wicked problems it has so far avoided. Indeed it must be the place of renewed civic society, in partnership with government, to ensure that the state is able to handle politics becoming difficult.

Life in 2060: A New Vision?

But what of a new vision? What can we do with the great power and riches we have created? The wealth and economic power of the United States and Europe today exceeds that of the 1950s or even 1960s and yet the constraints on policy making have created a political malaise. But back in the 1950s there was optimism about what we can do with the riches we create. It showed a potential destiny, a society and a world that would not only be richer but also better. What of the next five decades? What sort of economic destiny might we face?

A kind of 'tragedy of riches symposium' created to echo that of December 1950 was assembled. Drawn from politics, business, academia and journalism and including both those who feature in the story of this book and the generation which will be faced with delivery, some of the interesting projections of the future are as follows.

For Duncan Green of Oxfam, the charity which contrasted global poverty with the sums used to bail out the banks, there were two visions of the future: one rosy, the other gloomy. The optimistic first. 'At the beginning of the 21st Century, leaders and societies responded just in time to the growing problem of climate change and resource constraints. A combination of large scale investment in new green technologies ('20 Manhattan projects'), and the creation of a number of effective new global institutions meant that global carbon emissions were brought under control without interrupting the progress of poor countries. As a result, dollar a day poverty was eliminated by 2030, and something resembling a 20th Century welfare state created at a global level, with a global basic income guarantee, and universal education and healthcare. There remains plenty to do, however. The growing inadequacy of GDP as a measure of achievement has led to a shift to measuring and prioritizing human wellbeing, with a range of new economic and social metrics governing decision-making. Inequality remains a worry, as does conflict in a small (but shrinking) number of fragile states, but in terms of 20th Century development challenges, this looks like 'mission accomplished, what's next?' Oxfam decided to declare victory and close down at its 100th anniversary celebrations in 2042, and eventually closed its doors in 2050.'

John Williamson who coined the phrase The Washington Consensus, was 'willing to offer a hostage to fortune as I'll be long dead', nevertheless expected 'people in 2060 to be overwhelmed by the prospect of the planet getting hopelessly hot and cursing the people of our generation who sat back and enjoyed the good life that is now possible'.

This is a view echoed from a younger generation in Anya Kamenetz, who puts it starkly: 'The great wealth of the 20th century is global, industrial, and built through extraction. The challenge is to take advantage of the moment's relative, though declining, stability to reinvest those gains in creating sustainable, local, equitable economies. I see signs of this happening and a shift in values among many young people, but I don't know whether we can take advantage of social media and other emerging technologies to catalyze this shift before Nature comes to cash the cheque we have written on her'.

For Toby Ord, 'the possibilities we find most interesting have turned out to be ones where we think that their occurrence is less likely than not, but where their effects would be so large that we should pay attention to the possibility anyway. An example of this is machine intelligence which far exceeds the human level in most areas: this is far from certain to happen, but we can't be confident that it won't happen and the effects would be very dramatic (for good or for ill).' He goes on to consider the state of the world: 'I'm not sure whether or not the world will be more balanced, but I think that possible improvements would not be large enough to completely remove the need for aid. This doesn't mean that there won't be large improvements for the world's poorest people – for example, there have been large improvements in the quality of life of the poor people in developed countries, but redistributive taxation is still very useful as the gap between the rich and poor remains wide'.

In 2060, I suppose, people will, as they always do, appreciate most what too many of them will be lacking', forecasts former German Minister Erhard Eppler, 'Enough clean water, tomatoes which taste like tomatoes, people they can trust, a family which holds together, a town with a low crime rate, a house with little electronic noise, good teachers for their children, a competent health service and reliable social security and, last not least, a state that either provides this or allows people to provide it for themselves.

But Duncan Green returned with a gloomy vision which warns us of the dangers of complacency: 'The failure of the Copenhagen climate summit in 2009 and the subsequent collapse of the Kyoto process came to be seen as the end of the 'age of development' that saw unprecedented progress on health, education and income levels from the mid 20th Century afterwards. What followed was (and is) an 'age of scarcity' in which humanity has struggle to cope with growing resource constraints - soil, water, atmospheric space, increasingly erratic climatic conditions, and the inability of the post-World War Two global order to cope with the rise of new powers (China, India, Brazil and Indonesia). The age of scarcity has seen many more resource conflicts, both at national and international level, and a failure to contain climate change. Decades of progress in reducing poverty and hunger went into reverse. The tropical belt of the world has warmed by an average of four degrees, leading to collapsing rural economies, increased humanitarian disasters and millions of climate refugees attempting to flee to the well defended shores of the more temperate countries, There they confront what some have called a 'carbon curtain' of immigration controls. While suffering some of the consequences, both new and old powers have largely managed to adapt to the new, unstable climate conditions, although the rise in sea levels is causing massive disruptions of their economies. The same cannot be said for those left outside the carbon curtain. Oxfam's insistence on raising these issues saw it shut down by government decree in 2050'.

And what of this book's modest predictions? It must be clear by now that for democracy to remain relevant, a political strand will be needed by 2060 to complete the mixed economic settlement. The pendulum shift of global power from West to East, confirmed by our own global economic crisis, means that sooner or later politics will need to demonstrate a cultural change, adapting to our uncertain world. In the future, politics will need to take the difficult decisions that are avoided today. It will need to accept unwelcome policies through a 'veil of ignorance' in genuine partnership. And it will need to be able to articulate the purpose of our riches. The alternative is unpalatable.

These competing visions, some more optimistic than others, do not have to be the purpose of our riches or indeed the focus of policy. But there is a very real need to broaden our destiny wider than simply expanding our riches yet further. These new futurologists are strangely more world weary than their counterparts of the 1950s but are also perhaps more aware of the great economic power at our fingertips and also the constraints on using it. At the very least, though, they demonstrate that there really are possibilities for a new vision of what we can achieve.

Completing the Project: New Politics for a New Purpose

While it has been concerned with policy and wealth, this book is essentially interested in the political rather than a dusty economic response to the tragedy of our riches. It has argued that the mixed economic settlement - that blend of economic, welfare and social liberalism - is an incomplete project. While cementing its legacy, the two decades after the collapse of the Berlin Wall failed to provide the essential fourth corner to the endeavour and in its failure allowed our economic destiny to be squeezed. The completed project now requires a political settlement. This need is obscured by the reality that there is near universal mainstream political consensus about the mixed economic settlement as it stands. But consensus about this combined with tribal, party political competition means collusion between politicians and voters about dealing with the wicked problems. We have fooled ourselves into believing we can have mutually exclusive outcomes. And politicians are gleefully hypocritical in criticising their opponents for actions they themselves would take. It is the unsustainable cheat that, as politics becomes more difficult, is reaching breaking point.

A new punctuation in the incremental equilibrium of policy is desperately needed to allow politics to do the difficult things. But this cannot be simply about process. Systematic reform, while important, is not an end in itself; it must deliver a better politics and it must take people with it. Just as those examples of the Tea Party movement at grassroots level in the USA and the British coalition at executive level show, partnerships need to be formed. But to work they need to be formed in two directions: across the political spectrum and through society upwards, connecting to all types of communities and creating viable partnerships. The fourth strand must move to a post-majoritarianism politics which is fair and is sufficiently brave to tackle difficult and unpopular decisions in partnership. And in moving beyond simple tribalism we might even rediscover ideology in policymaking because the case will have to be made and the solution believed if it is to command widespread support and understanding. Different from the ideological battles of the past, this must be about combining and forming common visions; not dividing and ruling.

Only a new politics will provide a new economic destiny as optimistic as those from the 1950s or as brutally realistic as today's symposium. Our broader ambitions of just what we do with our riches must surely encompass our own wealthy societies and the harsh wider world. Along the way, this book has suggested that improved wellbeing, stronger communities, realistic democratic involvement, developing an understanding of fairness, properly tackling the environmental crisis, being prepared to interact with the poorer, emerging, world on fair economic terms, could form part of this destiny.

Conclusion: A Challenge to Politics

If this book is nothing else then it is a challenge to our own generation of politicians to fix our politics and redraw our economic destiny. But politics has to be more than something done to us; it has to comprise communities, ideas, umbrella groups as well as traditional parties.

The book has outlined the tragedy of our riches. It has described how the post war period formed a mixed economic settlement of welfare, social and economic liberalism. It is a settlement which as the Berlin Wall fell, almost all mainstream Western politicians accepted philosophically and pragmatically. And, during the decades of acceptance they instilled the settlement into policy. Over this period too, our great wealth was reconciled. After all, in Europe and the United States we enjoy a standard of living which separates us not only from the vast majority of the poorest in the world but also of our recent ancestors. The riches we have accumulated have provided for unparalleled consumerism, waste and ultimately unfulfilled wellbeing. It is clear to all that we do not live in the kind of advanced paradise that the futurologists of the 1950s predicted. This is not the fault of capitalism; it is the fault of near sighted politicians colluding with voters who are told they can have the irreconcilable. It is for this reason that a new, political, strand is needed to complete the mixed economic settlement.

235

This book does not critique markets as many popular books over recent years have done; it does not argue that open markets are some sort of evil creed. It does not blame capitalism. Neither does it argue that the panacea is ever more state intervention. It does, however, make the case that we have spent twenty years limiting just what capitalism can do for us. With the global ideological battles of the cold war behind us, the generation of politicians of the 1990s and the new millennium failed to update the vision, failed in political engagement and failed to take the most difficult of decisions. And the rhetorical response to the global economic downturn shows that little has changed in the second decade. Prosperity was and remains an end in itself. The creation and maintenance of riches is now the measure of successful policy making. And yet policy choices are constrained and there remain great wicked problems which require the attention of governments and crucially people. Our political system as it has developed is incapable of tacking the issues facing us all in the second decade of the twenty first century. Something needs to change. The starting point is to assess our great riches and answer a simple question:

What is it for?

Afterword

There is a great deal of difference in believing something still and believing it again.
W.H. Auden

The early reaction to the argument at the heart of this book has been more positive than I could have imagined. Friends and colleagues who read a draft version of this work (and from across the political spectrum) enthusiastically embraced the thesis. It seems that even where there are differences of opinion, the central instinct that we have lost our way over the past two decades rings true and that there is so much more that our rich societies can achieve. Some initial critiques, however, suggested that the book did not sufficiently elaborate upon the very same new vision of the future for which it so vehemently argues or indeed describe the structural nature of the new political settlement.

In the final chapter of the book, I hope I have offered some clues as to how we might move forward in embracing a new strand to the settlement and a new economic destiny. A political strand is needed which will see post-majoritarian political partnerships across traditional politics driven up from communities and creating sustainable and longer-term coalitions of ideas. A new destiny must be broader in terms of what capitalism can do for our wellbeing and fairness, right across the world. Nevertheless, I accept and acknowledge the deficiency but would make three crucial qualifications.

The first is that this book set out to make the case for just why change is needed and to explain how we got to this position with a broad contextual analysis. While some readers will disagree with its interpretation of evidence at times, it is hoped that most will recognise the need to meet the challenges the book sets out. The second reason is that the book was never conceived as a kind of blueprint for the change required; not least because a central argument of the work is that any new settlement must grow out of communities and be owned beyond the state and traditional tribal party politics. That is not to say that the nature of post-majoritarian politics nor the specifics of a new economic destiny are not important – they most certainly are – but this book serves a modest contribution to that great debate and hopefully the beginning of a constructive and lively conversation. To this end, I have set up a site (*policydiagnostics.com*) which I hope readers will use to exchange ideas, arguments and solutions. After all, getting involved is a principle of broadening our economic destiny. I hope you will get in touch and join the dialogue.

There is, however, a third reason. I believe the issues raised in this book are important and that we are now close to the point where traditional politics breaks down. The solution deserves real attention. The argument developed throughout and the spark of ideas in the final chapter of this book are a natural lead into a sequel to *Tragedy of Riches*. I have already begun researching and writing this and believe that some of the ideas, already in their infancy, will be surprising to those who read them.

I would like to thank all of those who have helped make this book what it is with comments, advice and support. Particular thanks go to Dr Etienne Khayat, Shiv Sinha and of course Maria Barber. I am also grateful to Christopher Woodhead and his colleagues at the University of Buckingham Press for getting this work into print.

Stephen Barber, London, 2011

References

Chapter 1

[1] Auden, W.H. 'The Unknown Citizen', first published in *The New Yorker* in 1939.

[2] Crafts, N and Toniolo, G. 'European Economic Growth 1950-2005: an overview', Discussion paper 6863, centre for Economic policy Research, June 2008. P3

[3] Badinger, H. 2005, 'Growth Effects of Economic Integration: Evidence from the EUMember States', *Review of World Economics*, 141, 50-78

[4] Crafts and Toniolo op cit, P19.

[5] See Wallace, W. 2001. Europe, the necessary partner. *Foreign Affairs,* 80, 16-34.

[6] Meyer, H. 'The Framework for Advancing Transatlantic Economic Relations', *Global Policy Institute Policy Pape*r 6, June 2008. P14.

[7] Haseler, S. 2004, *Super-State: the new Europe and its challenge to America*, IB Tauris. P126

[8] Kay, J. 2003, The *Truth About Markets: why some nations are rich but most remain poor*, Penguin. P 329

[9] See Brassey A. and Barber S.(ed), 2009 *Greed* , Palgrave Macmillan.

[10] Wall, D. 2005, *Babylon and Beyond: the economics of anti-capitalist, anti-globalist and radical green movements*, Pluto Press. P42

[11] Galbraith, J.K. 2004, *The Economics of Innocent Fraud*, Penguin. P 9.

[12] Sorman, G. 'Economics does not lie', *City Journal*, Summer 2008. The article and accompanying book attracted considerable debate. It

is also notable, given its publication date for the comment that 'the time of major global economic crises seems to have passed.'

[13] Kay, J. 2003, op cit. P 323.

[14] *Income, Poverty and Health Insurance Coverage in the United States: 2008*, US Census Bureau, September 2009.

[15] *2009 Annual Survey of Hours and Earnings*, ONS, November 2009. Taking 'full time' workers the increase should not be over-interpreted since post-recession there was a move toward part-time work.

[16] *CIA World Factbook*

[17] *United Nations World Statistics Pocketbook*, 2008.

[18] *Annual work hours per worker*, 2004, OECD,

[19] Aguiar, M. and Hurst, E. 'Measuring Trendsin Leisure: the allocation of time over five decades', *Working Paper 0-62*, Federal Reserve Bank of Boston. January 2006.

[20] O'Hara, M. and Anderson, W.T. 'Welcome to the Postmodern World' *Networker*, September/October 1991.

[21] Inglehart, R. 'Globalization and Postmodern Values', *The Washington Quarterly,* 23.1, 2000. P 215-228

[22] *Yearning for Balance: views of Americans on consumption, materialism and the Environment*, The Harwood Group (prepared for the Merck Family Fund) July 1995.

[23] Statistics taken from www.worldwatch.org.

[24] Schlosser, E. 2001, *Fast Food Nation: the dark side of the all-American meal*, Houghton.

[25] Survey report published by Italian commerce association Confcommercio Dec 2009.

[26] 'How Experts Think We'll Live in 2000 AD', *Robesonian (NC) / Associated Press*, 27/12/50. This and many other articles used in this research were accessed from www.paleofuture.com which is a fascinating site well worth a visit.

[27] Speaking on a 1966 radio documentary, *2000 AD: a documentary on life in the universe in the 21st Century,* hosted by Chet Huntley

[28] 'Little Work, Big Pay Forecast Year 2000', *Progress Index*, 30/7/69

[29] John F. Kennedy, *First Inaugural Address*, 20/1/61

Chapter 2

[1] Barack Obama G20 Press Conference 2/4/09, Transcript reproduced on *cbsnews.com*,

[2] 'Bank bailout could end poverty for 50 years – Oxfam tells G20', *Oxfam International*, 1/4/09, www.oxfam.org/en/pressroom. Last accessed Jan 2010

[3] Krugman, P. 2000, *The Return of Depression Economics*, Penguin. P161

[4] *Sinking & Swimming: understanding Britain's unmet needs*, Young Foundation Report , 2009. P28

[5] Rosenberg, N and Birdzell, L.E. 1986, *How the west Grew Rich: the economic transformation of the industrial world*, Basic Books.

[6] Brassey, A. 'What Drives Man Toward Greed?, in Brassey and Barber op cit. P 99.

[7] Rifkin, J. 2004, *The European Dream*, Polity. P 13.

[8] Calculation made by www.givingwhatwecan.org (last accessed December 2009). Dataset of world income distribution by Branko Milanovic, based on the year 2002, adjusted for inflation up to 2009 and using the new PPP ratings. It is not yet published, but it builds upon his data from 'True world income distribution, 1988 and 1993: First calculation based on household surveys alone', *Economic Journal* issue 112, 2002, p 75. According to the site, ''typical' to refer to the 'median', so the typical person is the one who earns more than half the world's population and less than the other half.'

[9] See www.globalrichlist.com, all subsequent numbers taken from here. Calculations from this site are based on figures from the *World Bank Development Research Group*. They assume the world's total

population is 6 billion and the average worldwide annual income is $5,000.

[10] Wolff, E. N. (2009). Recent trends in household wealth in the U.S., update to 2007: Rising debt and the middle class squeeze. *Working Paper in progress.* Annandale-on-Hudson, NY: The Levy Economics Institute of Bard College [look up ref]

[11] Haseler, S. 2010, *Meltdown: there is another way*, Forum Press. p37

[12] Ibid p 42

[13] *The Fidelity Millionaire Outlook Survey,* 2011.

[14] *World Economic Outlook*, IMF, April 2010.

[15] Sachs, J. 2006, *The End of Poverty: economic possibilities for our time,* Penguin.

[16] *Ministerial Salaries factsheet M6*, House of Commons Information Office, May 2009

[17] *Bank of England Annual Report 2007*, p29

[18] See *The Independent*, 21/10/09

[19] See Barber, S. 'Bonus brouhaha overshadows real problems', *FT Investment Adviser*, 9/11/09

[20] Arlidge, J. 'I'm doing 'god's work'. Meet Mr Goldman Sachs', Sunday Times, 8/11/09

[21] See for instance, Gilleard, C. and Higgs, P. 2005, *Contexts of Ageing,* Polity Press.

[22] Kamenetz, A. 2006, *Generation Debt: why now is terrible to be young,* Riverhead. P4

[23] Willets, D. 2010, T*he Pinch: how the baby boomers took their children's future and why they should give it back*, Atlantic Books.

[24] Haq, G. Minx, J. Whitelegg, J. Owen, A.2007, *Greening the Greys: climate change and the over 50s*, Stockholm Environment Institute.

[25] Stevenson, J. and Cook, C. 1977, *The Slump: society and politics during the depression*, Jonathan Cape. P5

[26] Gray, N. 1985, *The Worst of Times: an oral history of the great depression,* Wildwood House. P64

[27] Ibid p 68

[28] Shirer, W.L. 1971, *The Rise and Fall of the Third Reich: a history of Nazi Germany*, BCA. P136.

[29] Gray, C. 'Streetscapes: Central Park's 'Hooverville'; Life along Depression street', *New York Times*, 29/8/93

[30] Stephen A. Marglin and Juliet B. Schor (Eds), 1992, *The Golden Age of Capitalism: reinterpreting the postwar experience*, Oxford University Press.

[31] Skidelsky, R. 2009, Keynes: return of the master,

[32] Maddison, A. 2001, *The World Economy: A Millennial Perspective,* OECD.

[33] There remains confusion as to whether he was indeed assassinated or accidentally shot by his bodyguards.

[34] Long, H.P., *Share Our Wealth*, radio speech, NBC, 7/3/35

[35] Ravillion, M and Chen, S. 2008, *The Developing World is Poorer than we thought, but no less successful in the Fight Against Poverty*, World Bank working paper series 4703

[36] 'UK Elderly Fourth Poorest in EU', *BBC.co.uk*, 27/7/09

[37] Reproduced in McSmith, A.'First Among unequals', *The Independent*, 30/6/10

[38] Wilkinson, R. and Pickett, K. 2010, *The Spirit Level: why equality is better for everyone*, Penguin. P18

[39] Ibid. P25

[40] Young Foundation report, op cit P116

[41] Reiman, J. and Leighton, P. 2010, *The Rich Get Richer and the Poor go to Prison: ideology, class and criminal justice*, Allyn and Bacon/Pearson. P98

[42] Ibid p111

[43] *The Spirit Level* op cit. P5.

[44] Young Foundation report, op cit. P103

Chapter 3

[1] A sympathetic take on this was made by the British journalist Martin Kettle, 'The biggest problem for the Liberal Democrats is illiberal Britain', *The Guardian*, 10/9/09. The 2010 general election campaign saw Liberal Democrat stock soar temporarily only to be tempered on polling day. Nevertheless the balanced parliament which followed led to the first British coalition government since the second world war with Lib Dem policies central to the programme.

[2] Russell, C. 1999, *An Intelligent Person's Guide to Liberalism*, Gerald Duckworth & Co.

[3] To steal a phrase from the organisational culture literature. Deal T. and Kennedy, A. 2000, *Corporate Culture: the rites and rituals of corporate life*, Perseus Publishing.

[4] *Revenue Statistics 1965-2007*, OECD 2008, p48

[5] David Lloyd George had argued for the introduction of National Insurance as early as 1911 and had been a radical Chancellor introducing support for the incapacitated building on earlier H.H. Asquith's pension reforms. His radical 1909 Budget proposed re-distribution of wealth and was held up by the House of Lords. It led to two general elections in 1910 and the Parliament Act of 1911, limiting the power of the Lords. However, as Prime Minister after the war, great social reform failed to materialise.

[6] Hennessy, P. 1993, *Never Again*, Penguin . p2

[7] Education is notable in that it was an initiative of the Conservative Education secretary RAB Butler during the coalition government.

[8] Beveridge, W. 1953, *Power and Influence*, Hodder and Stoughton

[9] See Marr, A. *The History of Modern Britain*, BBC TV, 2009.

[10] 'The Politics of Death', *The Economist*, 3/9/09

[11] Dell, E. 1997, *The Chancellors: a history of the chancellors of the exchequer 1945-90*, Harper Collins. P 439

[12] Joseph, K.1975, *Reversing the Trend: A Critical Reappraisal of Conservative Economic and Social Policies*, Barry Rose.

[13] See. Jackson, P.M."Economic Policy, in Marsh D. and Rhodes, R.A.W. 1992, op cit. PP13-14. Coutts K. and Godley,W. 'The British Economy Under Mrs Thatcher', *Political Quarterly,* Vol. 60, 1989. pp 137-139.

[14] *1979 Conservative Party General Election Manifesto*

[15] Panic, M. 'Comment', in Michie, J. 1992, *The Economic Legacy 1979-1992*, Academic Press. P 58.

[16] Gilmour, I. 1992, op cit. P 21-22. Other commentators put the rise at 4%. Jackson, op cit. P 17.

[17] Hutton, W. 1996, op cit. P 70.

[18] Ibid. P 18-19. Martin, op cit. P 132.

[19] Marsh and Rhodes, op cit. P 177.

[20] Senker, P. 'Ten Years of Thatcherism: Triumph of ideology over economics', *Political Quarterly*, Vol. 60. 1989. P 181.

[21] Coutts and Godley, op cit. P 150.

[22] Gilmouropcit. P185.

[23] Thatcher MSS, RR to MT 30/4/75. Believed to be their first personal correspondence.

[24] Margaret Thatcher eulogy to Ronald Reagan, Washington, 11/6/04

[25] Reproduced in 'Reagan and Thatcher, Political Soul Mates', Associated Press, 5/6/04

[26] Reagan obituary, Tom Curry, MSNBC, 5/6/04

[27] Gilmour, I. 1993. op cit. P216

[28] Paton, P, 'Blair and the NHS' in Casey, T (ed), 2009, *The Blair Legacy: politics, policy, governance and foreign affairs*, Palgrave Macmillan. P110

[29] Incidentally, new right conservatives in the United States similarly derided the achievements of President Johnson which led to black rights in a country which had segregation and prevalent white supremacists.

[30] Tony Blair outlining the key themes of Labour's five year plan on law and order. 19/7/04

[31] Amusingly in his memoirs, Blair's admonishment of himself for allowing the Freedom of Information Act read: 'You idiot. You naive, foolish, irresponsible nincompoop.' Blair, T. 2010, *A Journey*, Hutchinson.

[32] Interview with Robin Day. Op cit. P65

[33] Ibid P66

[34] Germany, K. 'War on Poverty' *University of Virginia Readings* 2005. P3

[35] At 45 he was the youngest Home Secretary since Churchill in 1910 but at an age which today would seem to be standard for political leadership.

[36] Jenkins book published in 1959 was titled *Is Britain Civilised?* See Diamond, P. 2004, *New Labour's Old Roots*, Imprint.

[37] Interview with Robin Day op cit. P63

[38] Ibid.

Chapter 4

[1] Bill Clinton was far from the first US President to commit adultery or display other low morals but even the 'Camelot' of Kennedy maintained a strict level of privacy to which the Clinton White House could only dream. See Robert Dallek, 2003, *John F. Kennedy: an unfinished life*, Penguin.

[2] Bill Clinton inauguration speech,31/3/92

[3] Klein, J. 2002, *The Natural: the misunderstood Presidency of Bill Clinton*, Broadway. P 9

[4] Bill Clinton, *First Inaugural Address*, Washington DC, 20/1/93

[5] The original teasing news report had been Andrew Rosenthal, 'Bush Encounters the Supermarket, Amazed', *New York Times*, 5/2/92. 'The he grabbed a quart of milk, a light bulb and a bag of candy and ran them over an electronic scanner. The look of wonder flickered across his face again as he saw the item and price registered on the cash register screen'.

[6] Major, J. 1999, *The Autobiography*, Harper Collins

[7] Ramsden, J. 'Leadership and Change: prime ministers in the post-war world – Edward Heath', *Gresham College Lecture*, Gresham College London, 21/3/96

[8] Tony Blair speaking before the Chicago Economic Club setting out the 'doctrine of the international community', 22/4/99.

[9] Samuel, H. 'Nicolas Sarkozy blames the generation of 1968', *The Telegraph*, 29/4/08

[10] 'The war of French dressing', *The Economist*, 14/1/10

[11] Haseler, S, 2004, *Super-State: the new Europe and its challenge to America*, IB Tauris. P 38

[12] Blair, *A Journey*, op ct.. P 228

[13] See Meyer H. and Barber, S. 'Making Transatlantic Economic relations Work', *Global Policy*, Jan 2011..

[14] Fukuyama, F. 1993, The *End of History and the Last Man*, Harper Perennial

[15] Gray, J. 1999, *False Dawn: the delusions of modern capitalism*, Granta. p103-4

[16] Sorman 2008 op cit.

[17] Zizek op cit.P3

[18] Ibid p5

[19] Giddens, A. 1994, *Beyond Left and Right: the future of radical politics*, Polity. Giddens, A. 1995, *Politics, Sociology and Social Theory: encounters with classical and contemporary social thought*, Polity.

[20] Joe Biden speaking at the *CNN Democratic Debate*. 15/11/07

[21] Barack Obama, Presidential announcement, 10/2/07, Springfield Illinois

[22] Kahn, J. 'Leaders for a New Age', *Newsweek*, 12/1/08

[23] Canellos, P. 'Obama's new breed of baby boomer', *The Boston Globe*, 20/2/07

[24] See for instance, Barnes, E. 'Clegg anger over 'ageism against Ming', *Scotland on Sunday*, 21/10/07.

[25] Lord Liverpool was 42 when he became First Lord of the Treasury in 1812. How long will it be before that record is beaten and the records look back to Pitt?

[26] Barber, S.'Managing Departments of State', *Professional Manager*, November 2006.

[27] *British Social Attitudes Survey*, 2010, National Centre for Social Research.

Chapter 5

[1] See Greenwald, J. 'Greenspan's Rates of Wrath', *Time Magazine*, 28/11/94

[2] Lindblom, C.E., 1965, *The Intelligence of Democracy: decision-making through mutual adjustment*, Free Press.

[3] A piece worth looking up here is Cyert, R and March, J. 1963, *A Behavioral Theory of the Firm*, Englewood Cliffs. For a broader analysis of strategy in the context of political science, see Barber, S. 2005, *Political Strategy: modern politics in contemporary Britain*, Liverpool Academic Press.

[4] Hayes, M. 2001, *The Limits of Policy Change: incrementalism, worldview and the rule of law*, Georgetown University Press. P4.

[5] See for instance Kiel, D and Elliott, E. 'Budgets as Dynamic Systems: change, variation, time, and budgetary heuristics, *Journal of Public Administration Research and Theory*, 1992, 2:1. .

[6] Baumgartner, F and Jones, B. 1993, *Agendas and Instability in American Politics*, University of Chicago Press.

[7] *The Demographic Future of Europe – from challenge to opportunity*, EU Legislative summary, europa.eu.

[8] See Population Newsletter, Department of Economic and Social Affairs, UN, June 2008

[9] See Golub, P. 2010, *Power, Profit and Prestige: a History of American Imperial Expansion*, Pluto.

[10] Mulgan, G. 'After Capitalism', *Prospect Magazine*, 26/4/09

[11] Huber, J and Skidmore, P. 2003, *The New Old: why the baby boomers won't be pensioned off*, Demos; Harkin, J and Huber,J. 2004, *Eternal Youths: How the baby boomers are having their time again*, Demos.

[12] Harkin and Huber op cit. P13.

[13] Biggs, S, Phillipson, C, Leach, R, and money, A. 2006, 'Baby Boomers and Adult Aging in Public Policy', *Cultures of Consumption Working Paper 27*, Birkbeck College. P18

[14] *Young Voters in the 2008 Presidential Election*, CIRCLE factsheet, Dec 2008.

[15] Friedman, T.L. 2005, *The World is Flat: a brief history of the twenty-first century*, Farrar Straus Giroux.

[16] Martin, B. 1993, I*n the Public Interest?* Zed. P1

[17] Mishra, R. 1999, *Globalization and the Welfare State*, Edward Elgar.

[18] Campanella, M.L. 'The Effects of Globalization and Turbulence on Policy-Making Processes', *Government and Opposition*, vol 28 issue 2, April 1993.

[19] Amongst others see Polanyi, K. 2001, *The Great Transformation: the political and economic origins of our time*, Beacon Press.

[20] Jessop, B. (1994) 'The Transition to Post-Fordism and the Schumpeterian Workfare State', in Burrows, R. and Loader, B. (eds), 1994, *Towards a Post-Fordist Welfare State*. Routledge

[21] Dahrendorf, R. 'Preserving Prosperity', *New Statesman,* December 1995

[22] Gray, *False Dawn*, op cit. P78

[23] Greenspan, A. 2007, *The Age of Turbulence: adventures in a new world*, Allen Lane. P 365.

[24] Ibid.

[25] Kay, J. 2004, *The Truth About Markets*, Penguin. P308.

[26] Williamson, J. 1990, "What Washington Means by Policy Reform", in J. Williamson, ed., *Latin American Adjustment: How Much Has Happened?,* Institute for International Economics.

[27] Gray, *False Dawn*, op cit. P201

[28] Williamson, J "What Should the Bank think about the Washington Consensus?", speech to the Institute for International Economics July 1999.

[29] Gilpin, R. 1987, *The Political Economy of Industrial Relations*, Princeton University Press. P 289

[30] Soros, G. 2000, *Reforming Global Capitalism*, Little Brown.

[31] Stiglitz, J. 2002, *Globalization and its Discontents*, Penguin.

[32] Summary of the *United Nations Monetary and Financial Conference*, 22/7/44

[33] IMF Articles of Agreement, Article VI. Section 3, read: "Controls of capital transfers: Members may exercise such controls as are necessary to regulate international capital movements, but no member may exercise these controls in a manner which will restrict payments for current transactions or which will unduly delay transfers of funds in settlement of commitments…"

[34] Hutton, W. 2002, *The World We're In*, Little Brown. P 186; Stiglitz, J. op cit P 11.

[35] Daunton, M. 'Britain and Globalisation Since 1850: IV the creation of the Washington Consensus', *Transactions of the Royal Historical Society*, 2009. P 2.

[36] Stiglitz, op cit P 16

[37] Ibid.

[38] Taleb,N. 2007, *The Black Swan: the impact of the highly improbable*, Penguin. P xix

[39] See Barber's Regulatory Super-Cycle model, Barber, S. 'The Disputable Truth of Economic Greed', in Brassey and Barber (ed) op cit. P 89.

[40] Stiglitz, J. op cit.

[41] Mckee, M. and Benjamin, M. 'Stigliz says ties to Wall Street doom bank rescue', *Bloomberg News*, 17/4/09

[42] Dryzek, J and Dunleavy, P. 2010, *Theories of the Democratic State*, Palgrave Macmillan.

[43] Eppler, E., 2009, *Return of the State?*, Forum Press. P231

[44] See 'Voting Share at the IMF and World Bank in 2009', www.globalpolicy.org/component/content/article/104/46584.html

[45] See Conway, E. and Monaghan, A, 'Mervyn King Criticises Gordon Brown over Budget Deficit', *Telegraph*, 24/11/09

Chapter 6

[1]*The Mellon and Kennedy Tax Cuts: A Review and Analysis*, 1982, Joint Economic Committee.

[2] Knight, F.H. 'Economics, Political Science and Education', *The American Economics Review*, Vol 34, No 1, Part 2. 1944.

[3] 'Much Apu About Nothing', *The Simpsons*, season 7, episode 23, first aired 5/5/96

[4] Downs, A. 1957, *An Economic Theory of Democracy*, Harper & Row

[5] See Barber, S. 2005, *Political Strategy: modern politics in contemporary Britain*, Liverpool Academic Press.

[6] Dunleavy, P . 1991, *Democracy, Bureaucracy and Public Choice*, Harvester Wheatsheaf. P118.

[7] 'Breakfast with Frost' *BBC1*, 16/1/00.

[8] *Copenhagen Accord*, United Nations Framework Convention on Climate Change, 18/12/09

[9] Vidal, J. 'Carbon emissions will fall 3% due to recession, say world energy analysts', *The Guardian*, 6/10/09

[10] See Parker, B. 2005, *Introduction to Globalization and Business*, Sage p 161; Hodgson, S. 'Vested interests prevent agreement on climate change', *Energy World*, February 2010. P2.

[11] Giddings, B. Hopwood, B. and O'Brien, G. 'Environment, Economy and Society: fitting them together into sustainable development', *Sustainable Development*, Vol 10, 2002.

[12] Mill, J.S 2005, *On Liberty*, Cosimo Classics

[13] Or for that matter Blair, Brown and Bush since Mill believed that causing offence did not constitute harm, and therefore advocated near total freedom of speech.

[14] Blattberg, C. 'Political Philosophies and Political Ideologies', *Public Affairs Quarterly*, Vol 15, No. 3, July 2001

[15] Eysenck, H.1961,*Sense and Nonsense in Psychology*, Pelican.

[16] Nolan, D. 'Classifying and Analyzing Politico-Economic Systems', *The Individualist*, January 1971.

[17] In 2005, Maya Anne Evans was arrested and convicted of unauthorised protest for reading out names at the Cenotaph of British soldiers killed in the Iraqi invasion; that same year, 82 year old Walter Wolfgang, a Jewish Nazi escapee and Labour party member was arrested at the Labour party conference for shouting 'rubbish' at Foreign Secretary Jack Straw. In the United States in 2003, Stephen Downs was arrested in a New York shopping mall under trespass law for refusing to remove T-shirts with the slogans 'Give Peace a Chance' and 'Peace on Earth' while his son Roger was threatened with arrest for wearing a shirt that read 'Let the Inspections Work' and 'No War With Iraq.' They bought the garments in the mall. In France in 2004, Muslim school girls were sent home from school for wearing the hijab following the introduction of a law banning Islamic headscarves. In 2006, David Irving was sentenced by an Austrian court to three years imprisonment for holocaust denial, the sentence crucially influenced not only by his published past beliefs but crucially his current thoughts. In Germany during the 1990s, the philosopher Peter Singer's book, *Practical Ethics* (Cambridge University Press, 1979), was suppressed by angry and at times violent opinion since one of its ten chapters advocated euthanasia for severely handicapped newborn infants.

[18] British women 'of property' over the age of 30 got the vote in 1918, it took until 1928 for the voting age to be equal to men. Similar to most western democracies, American women won the vote in the 1920s, while French and Japanese women had to wait until 1945.

[19] The End of the Civil war and the Thirteenth Amendment to the US constitution abolished slavery in 1865. In response, many states enacted 'black codes' limiting the freedoms of former slaves. The fourteenth amendment countered these codes but, owing to the Supreme Court's unwillingness to enforce the fourteenth amendment, segregation continued until the Civil Rights Act of 1964.

[20] Rockey, J. 'Who is Left-Wing, and Who Just Thinks They Are?', *Working Paper 09/23*, May 2010, University of Leicester.

[21] Oborne, P. 2005, *The Rise of Political Lying*, Free Press. P125

[22] Forbes 400 Richest People in America, Forbes.com, 17/9/08

[23] See Chan, S. 'Bloomberg Leaving Republican Party', *New York Times*, 19/6/07

[24] Mayor Michael Bloomberg speaking at *Ceasefire*, 18/6/07,

[25] Galbraith, J.K. 1992, *The Culture of Contentment*, Houghton Mifflin. P182

[26] Webb, P. 2007, *Democracy and Political Parties*, Hansard Society. P7

[27] Budge, I. and Keman, H. 1990, *Parties and Democracy*, Oxford University Press.

[28] According to a poll conducted by MPR in Minnesota during May 2010, 20% of electorate supported the Tea party Movement with some 50% stating that it 'doesn't reflect my views'.

[29] *Fox News* 24/5/10.

[30] Fifield, A. 'Tea party Candidates Threaten US Poll Upset', *Financial Times*, 13/8/10

[31] Mainwaring, D. 'Tea Party's Inception a Rebirth', *Washington Times*, 13/8/10

[32] See Thompson, K. and Balz, D. 'Rand Paul Comments about Civil Rights Stir Controversy', *Washington Post*, 21/5/10

[33] 'Hardtalk with Andrew Neil', *BBC News*, 24, 29/5/10

[34] 'Five Days that Changed Britain', *BBC2*, first shown 29/7/10

[35] Emma Reynolds MP talking at a seminar. Organised by BBC World Service 'Coalition: lessons from the World.' Committee Room 6, House of Commons, 21/7/10.

[36] John Major, evidence before the Public Administration Committee, 10/11/09. He was talking about his opposition to coalition governments.

[37] Speaking on 'The Andrew Marr Show', *BBC1*, 8/8/10

[38] Hayek, F. 1978, *The Constitution of Liberty*, University of Chicago Press. p31

[39] Littlewood, M. 'Hack away – and smile while doing it, minister', *Sunday Times*, 5/9/10.

[40] Hayek, F, Letter to *The Times*, 11/7/78

[41] Birrell, I. 'Big Society? Let me Explain', *The Guardian*, 9/10/10

[42] Norman, J. 2010, *The Big Society: the anatomy of the new politics*, University of Buckingham Press. P6

[43] See Barber, S. and Oldfield, C. 'Is the Big Society Just another Stakeholder Society?', Paper given to *IRSPM Conference*, Dublin, April 2011.

[44] *Woman's Own*, 23/10/87

[45] Norman, 2010, op cit. p 195.

[46] 'Generations in Balance', *New York Times*, 18/6/10

Chapter 7

[1] Frank, R.H. 2000, *Luxury Fever: money and happiness in an era of excess*, Princeton University Press. p3-4

[2] Report author, Professor Ronald Kessler of Harvard points out that Americans are more likely to talk about depression and that 'in Nepal, for instance, mentally ill people can be put in jail because of a

lack of mental health facilities.' See Van Dusen, A. 'How Depressed is your Country?', *Forbes Magazine*, 16/2/07.

[3] Seligman, M. E. P. in Buie, J. 'Me' decades generate depression: individualism erodes commitment to others'. *APA Monitor*, 19, 18, 1988. 'People born after 1945 were ten times more likely to suffer from depression than people born 50 years earlier.'

[4] Stiglitz, J. 2003, *The Roaring Nineties: why we're paying the price for the greediest decade in history*, Penguin. P5

[5] Greenspan, 2007 op cit. P 363

[6] Hall, B. 'France to Count Happiness in GDP, *Financial Times*, 14/9/09

[7] Report by Commission on the Measurement of Economic Performance and Social Progress, op cit. p12

[8] Ibid P13

[9] Easterlin, R. 'Does economic growth improve the human lot? Some empirical evidence', in David P. and Rede, M. (eds), 1974, *Nations and Households in Economic Growth: essays in honor of Moses Abramovitz*, Academic Press NY.

[10] Ibid p 118

[11] Hagerty M. and Veenhoven, R. 'Wealth and Happiness Revisited: growing wealth of nations does go with greater happiness', *Social Indicators Research*, Vol 64, 2003, pp1-27. There are further criticisms of their use of comparative data with poorer countries where comparative information is less comprehensive.

[12] Layard, R. 'Happiness: has social science a clue?', *Lionel Robbins Memorial Lecture*, 2003.

[13] Oswald, A. 'Happiness and Economic Performance', Economic Journal, 1997, vol 107. pp1815-31

[14] *The Spirit Level*, op cit. P6

[15] Sorman 2008 op cit.

[16] Galbraith, J.K. 1999, *The Affluent Society*, Penguin. P 1.

[17] See Wall op cit P189.

[18] Gregor, K. 'Broadband to become a human right in Finland', *The National Business Review*, 15/10/09

[19] *Universal Declaration of Human Rights*, 10/12/48

[20] http://www.ohchr.org/EN/UDHR/Pages/WorldRecord.aspx

[21] Moore's film production unearthed film footage of FDR's address previously thought lost.

[22] Roosevelt, F.D., 11/1/44, *State of the Union Address*.

[23] Ariens, C. 'Glenn Beck, a ratings hit for Fox, takes his show to the people', *TVNewser*, 6/3/09

[24] *Glenn Beck, Fox News, 26/10/09*

[25] *For Richer or Poorer: transforming economic partnership agreements between Europe and Africa*, Christian Aid, April 2005.

[26] *New Statesman* interview8/1/10

[27] Treanor, J. 'New outrage over billion-pound bonus plan at Barclays and RBS', *The Guardian*, 14/2/10

[28] 'Time to thin down fat cat pay', *Personnel Today*, 17/2/04

[29] Wearden, G.'UK boardroom pay leaps 55% in a year', *The Guardian*, 28/10/10

[30] Warren Buffett cited by Obama, B. 2008, *The Audacity of Hope*, P191

[31] Report on *Broadcasting House*, BBC Radio 4, 15/11/09

[32] Lewis, J. 'Toby Ord's philosophy is one we could all learn from', *Sunday Telegraph*, 21/11/09

[33] www.givingwhatwecan.org

[34] See Milan, M. 'Apple Removes $1000 featureless iPhone Application', *LA Times*, 7/8/08

[35] *The Spirit Level* op cit. P 30.

[36] Carter, J. 'Energy and the National goals: a crisis of confidence', address delivered 15/7/79.

[37] 'EU Effusion" lost in Translation"', *BBC.co.uk*, 27/3/07

[38] Margaret Thatcher, Speech to the Small Business Bureau Conference, 8/2/1984

[39] Walters, S. 'Sleepless Margaret Thatcher stayed up for entire Falklands war', *Daily Mail*, 29/11/09

[40] Keynes, J.M. 1972, *Essays in Persuasion, Vol IX, The Collected Works of John Maynard Keynes,* Cambridge University Press. p331

[41] Report by Commission on the Measurement of Economic Performance and Social Progress, op cit. P8

[42] Crawford, M. 2010, *The Case for Working with your Hands: or Why Office Work is bad for us and Fixing Things Feels Good*, Viking. P3.

Chapter 8

[1] Barber, S. discussant at Pixley, Jocelyn seminar paper, 'Perception Inflation: From Credibility Conflicts to Global Banking Crises', *Global Policy Institute*, 16/9/08

[2] Phillips, M. 'Is the Rescue Plan Socialism? The Far Left Says, 'No Way, Comrade'', *Wall Street Journal*, 4/20/08.

[3] Barack Obama, addressing joint session of Congress, 25/2/09

[4] Reproduced by the Financial Times online: http://ftalphaville.ft.com/blog/2009/03/12/53522/an-1897-boom-and-bust-retrospective

[5] Galbraith, J.K. 1961, *The Great Crash 1929*, Pelican. P21

[6] Rowthorn R. and Ramaswamy, R. 1997, *De-industrialisation: causes and implications*, IMF working paper. P6-7

[7] Darling, A. *Budget Speech*, House of Commons, 24/3/10

[8] Mombiot, G. Speaking on BBC Radio *Today Programme*, 18/5/10

[9] Proudhon, P. 'The Authority Principle' in Guerin, D. (ed), 2006, *No Gods, No Masters: An Anthology of Anarchism*, AK Press. P 55-56

[10] Nozick, R. 1988, *Anarchy, State and Utopia*, Blackwell. P169

[11] Rawls, J. 1973, *A Theory of Justice*, Oxford University Press. P 136-7

[12] Jochum, V. Pratten B. and Wilding, K. 2005, *Civil Renewal and Active Citizenship*, NCVO

Index

Africa 32, 41, 120, 194
American Dream 29
Attlee, Clement 52-55, 59, 65,
77, 174
Auden, W.H. 7, 237

Baby Boomers 34-36, 41, 82,
91-93, 101, 183
Banks and Bankers 33, 124,
125, 127, 129, 195-196,
210, 212, 216-217, 220
Beck, Glenn 193-194
Bentham, Jeremy 182
Berlin Wall 90, 106, 119, 150,
183, 232
Beveridge, William 54, 56-57,
59
Bhutan, Kingdom of 190
Biden, Joe 97-98
Big Society 176-178
Blair Doctrine 86-87
Blair, Tony 13, 65, 68, 71-72,
84-86, 87, 88, 91-93, 101,
128, 143, 149, 177
Bloomberg, Michael 161-162
Brassey, Alex 29
Bretton Woods 121-122
Brown, Gordon 25, 100, 123,
128, 213, 221
Bubbles (Asset) 215, 217
Buffett, Warren 197, 211, 226

Bush, George H W 84, 92
Bush, George W 13, 25, 88,
91-93, 128, 212

Cameron, David 100, 101, 167-
168, 176
CAP 194
Capitalism 2, 10, 11-13, 40, 52,
113, 193, 209, 213
Carter, Jimmy 200
Carville, James 105
Centre for Policy Studies 61
China 146, 196, 219, 231
Churchill, Winston 35, 52, 55,
86, 168
City of London 33, 64, 128,
196, 220
Civic Society 227
Civil Rights 19, 74, 155, 167,
202
Clegg, Nick 100, 167-168
Clinton, Bill 23, 58, 82-84, 88,
91-93, 105, 184, 227
Club of Rome 189
Coalition (UK) 167-169
Cold War 10, 106, 184
Conservative Party 53, 54-55,
60, 67, 69, 72, 101, 157,
167-168, 171-172, 176,
177
Consumerism 1, 15, 17, 34, 71,

115, 147, 181, 187, 199, 209
Criminal Justice System 45

Darling, Alistair 32, 222
Debt (National) 41, 109, 133, 211
Declaration of Independence 201
Deindustrialisation 20, 63, 142, 205, 218-220,
Demographics 111-113, 142
Depression (Economics) 37-38, 42, 53
Depression (Psychological) 183
Downs, Anthony 140-141
Dylan, Bob 71, 83

Earnings 15, 196, 198
Engel, Ernst 219
Entitlements 192-197
Environment 144-145, 154, 179, 221-223, 229-231
Eppler, Erhard 130-131, 230
Equality 10, 19, 44, 64, 155

Fairness 196, 223-226,
Friedman, Thomas 114-115
Fukuyama, Francis 94-95, 96
Futurology 19-20, 228-232

Galbraith, J.K. 12, 164, 190, 216
Gilmour, Ian 63, 65, 68
Global Economic Crisis (2008) 12, 25, 26, 96, 127-128,

135, 185, 209-214, 220
Globalisation 98, 106, 114, 116, 118-121, 128, 146, 184, 196
Grant Group 197-198
Gray, John 95, 117
Greenspan, Alan 118, 123, 128, 185
Growth 9, 40, 41, 62, 153, 187, 190, 213, 217, 229

Happiness 186-190, 200, 201, 204, 206
Hayek, Friedrich 11, 19, 26, 36, 38, 43, 46, 58-59, 78, 111, 134, 165, 194, 225
Heath, Edward 60, 67, 86
Hitler, Adolf 39
Hobbes, Thomas 150
Hooverville 39
Human Rights 192, 201
Hutton, Will 14, 123

IMF 60, 120, 127, 131
Incrementalism (Policy) 108, 156, 233
Inequality 15-16, 27, 43-44, 65, 118, 154, 220, 229
Iraq War 13, 88, 90

Jenkins, Roy 50, 73, 75-77, 86
Johnson, Lyndon B 22, 74
Joseph, Keith 60-61
Judt, Tony 179

Kamenetz, Anya 35, 229
Kay, John 11, 14, 119

Keane, John 139
Kennedy, John F 21-23, 73, 87, 198, 203
Keynes, John Maynard and Keynsianism 12, 40, 55, 56-57, 60, 122, 206, 209
King, Martin Luther 71
King, Mervyn 32, 133
Kosovo Intervention 93
Krugman, Paul 27

Labour Party 50, 52-53, 54, 56, 60, 65, 68-69, 72, 77, 91-92, 100-101, 149, 177, 221
Laffer Curve 137-138
Liberal Democrat Party 50, 76, 100, 167, 171
Liberalism 49-50, 72, 94, 150-151
Littlewood, Mark 175
Locke, John 151, 201
Long, Huey P 41-43

Macmillan, Harold 40, 55
Major, John 85, 92, 169, 185
Materialism 14, 16 ,45, 112, 118, 187, 200
Merkel, Angela 50, 142
Metropolis (1927) 18-19
Meyer, Henning 10
Miliband, Ed 100, 178
Mill, John Stuart 49, 72, 156
Monetarism 61
Moral Hazards 125
MTFS (1980) 62-63

Nationalisation 53, 129, 132

New Deal 42
New Public Management 69
NHS 53, 57, 65, 69, 77, 143
Nixon, Richard 22, 92, 123
Nolan Chart 152
Nozick, Robert 223-224

Obama, Barack 15, 27, 58, 98, 113, 127, 145, 179, 214
Ord, Toby 198, 230
Osborne, George 133
Oxfam 26, 226, 228-229, 231

Palin, Sarah 59, 166
Political Spectrum 148-152, 160
Post War Consensus 51, 55, 62, 65-66, 77
Post-majoritarianism 171
Poverty 26, 28, 32, 43, 44, 74, 189, 198, 228
Price, Katie 200
Privatisation 64, 65, 116, 120
Proudhon, Pierre Joseph 223-224
Punctuated Equilibrium (Policy) 109, 141, 156, 250

Rawls, John 225
Reagan, Ronald 23, 40, 66-68, 116, 137, 138, 170
Riots (London) i, 158, 227
Riots (Paris) 71
Roosevelt, Eleanor 202-203
Roosevelt, Franklin D 42, 49, 193, 202

Sachs, Jeffrey 32
Sarkozy, Nicolas 89, 186, 190-192
Schwartzenegger, Arnold 141
Second World War 8, 23, 27, 34-35, 37, 50, 81, 86, 168
Simpsons, The 139
Social Democracy 13, 51, 130
Sorman, Guy 14, 190
Soros, George 2, 121
Spirit Level, The 44, 46, 189
Stakeholder Society 177
Stiglitz, Joseph 2, 121, 126-127, 184, 186
Superpower 22, 57, 105, 119
Taleb, Nassim 124
Taxation 32, 42, 51, 62, 120, 128, 137, 179, 223-224
Tea Party 165-167, 173, 226, 233
Technology 20, 113, 184, 192, 221
Terrorist Attacks New York (2001) 13, 90, 162
Thatcher, Margaret 44, 55, 60-62, 64, 65, 66-68, 69, 77, 78, 116, 158, 168, 174, 177, 204-205, 219
Transatlantic Relationship 10, 11, 94
Tribalism 139, 159-160, 163, 168, 233
Truman, Harry S 210

Underclass 43-46
Unemployment 20, 37, 38, 40, 53, 58, 62, 193, 218

Values 10, 16, 17, 42, 95, 154-156, 159, 172, 230

Wall Street Crash (1929) 216
Washington Consensus 40, 119-121, 130
Wealth 9, 30-32, 45, 146, 148, 181, 199, 214
Webb, Paul 164
Welfare 51, 52-54, 57, 65, 143
Wellbeing 45, 182, 186-190
White, Harry Dexter 122
Willets, David 35, 172
Williamson, John 119, 229
Woodstock Festival 70
Work 11, 16, 20, 38, 45, 53, 114, 142, 185, 202, 220, 224
World Bank 43, 120, 123, 126-127, 131

Young Foundation 27, 45, 46

Zizek, Slavoj 2, 96